DISCARDED

BLACK HAWK MIDDLE SCHOOL
EAGAN, MN

D0848244

INDIA

ABDO
Publishing Company

INDIA

by A. M. Buckley

BLACK HAWK MIDDLE SCHOOL
EAGAN, MN

Content Consultant
Sumit Ganguly,
Rabindranath Tagore Professor of Indian Cultures
and Civilizations, Indiana University, Bloomington

CREDITS

Published by ABDO Publishing Company, 8000 West 78th Street, Edina, Minnesota 55439. Copyright © 2012 by Abdo Consulting Group, Inc. International copyrights reserved in all countries. No part of this book may be reproduced in any form without written permission from the publisher. The Essential Library™ is a trademark and logo of ABDO Publishing Company.

Printed in the United States of America,
North Mankato, Minnesota
062011
092011

 THIS BOOK CONTAINS AT LEAST 10% RECYCLED MATERIALS.

Editor: Melissa York
Copy Editor: Susan M. Freese
Series design and cover production: Emily Love
Interior production: Kazuko Collins

About the Author: A. M. Buckley is an artist, writer, and children's book author based in Los Angeles, California. She has written several books for children.

Library of Congress Cataloging-in-Publication Data
Buckley, A. M., 1968-
 India / by A.M. Buckley.
    p. cm. -- (Countries of the world)
 Includes bibliographical references and index.
 ISBN 978-1-61783-111-9
 1. India--Juvenile literature. I. Title.
 DS407.B83 2012
 954--dc22
                                        2011007944

Cover: Taj Mahal, Agra, India

TABLE OF CONTENTS

CHAPTER 1
A VISIT TO INDIA

You wake up to the Indian flight attendant announcing in her liltingly accented English that the plane will soon touch down in Mumbai. Seat belt securely fastened, you gaze out the window at the sparkling lights of India's large industrial center. You've seen a few Bollywood movies and eaten Indian food, but you know that these are only small elements of India's complex and diverse culture. What will India really be like? You take a deep breath, ready for anything.

It's still nighttime when you deplane at Chhatrapati Shivaji International Airport, which is also called by its old name, Sahar. You step into the warm air, hail one of the many black and yellow taxis waiting outside the airport, and zip through the night to the center of Mumbai. The capital of the western Indian state of Maharashtra awaits you.

India is home to 15 percent of Earth's population.

The Gateway of India beckons travelers into Mumbai.

Wide awake because you slept on the plane, you ask the driver to take you straight to Sassoon Dock in the Colaba district. As the sun rises over the Arabian Sea, you see busy fishers unloading their catches. On the dock, women wearing brightly colored saris pile fish, lobster, and shrimp into baskets. Then, balancing the baskets on their heads, the women make their way through the growing crowds of shopkeepers and restaurant owners who have come to bargain at the largest fish market in the city.

CHOR BAZAAR

Chor Bazaar, located in the heart of Mumbai, is one of many popular open-air markets in India. Also called by its English name, Thieves' Market, it is a hot spot for antique shoppers. There, shoppers search for relics from India's long history—everything from ancient figurines to Victorian furniture. Vendors also sell jewelry, carvings, watches, tea sets, and more. Nearby are the vegetable market, called the Null Bazaar, and the busy *kirana* (grain) market, where tons of grains are bought and sold each day.

From there, you make your way down the busy Colaba Causeway. The avenue is lined with modern shops selling electronics, sportswear, and designer items. All along the street, vendors in crowded stalls sell colorful beads, shiny pots, sticky sweets, and handmade crafts. You look at their wares but decide to save your shopping for the bazaar.

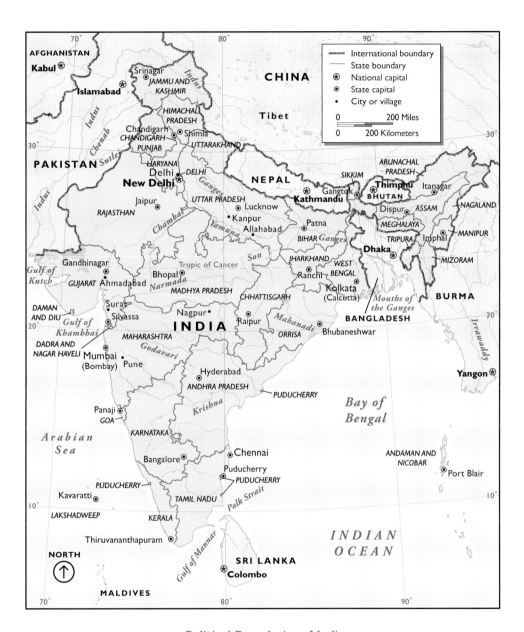

Political Boundaries of India

Later, you make your way toward Mumbai's most famous monument, the Gateway of India. The monument is bustling. Everywhere you look, you see colors and crowds. Local men, women, and children gather to visit and chat, and groups of tourists from all over the world come to admire the architecture and marvel at the city.

GATEWAY OF INDIA

This triumphant stone archway, made of yellow basalt and reinforced concrete, sits on the waterfront in South Mumbai. The main arch stretches 86 feet (26 m) into the sky. The stone is carved with intricate latticework, and the structure boasts four turrets. Originally made to commemorate the arrival of King George V and Queen Mary of England, the archway is also the place where the last of the British ships departed when colonial rule ended and India became independent.

As you wander through the sprawling streets, you pass ancient temples and glamorous hotels. You see other contrasts everywhere you look: street vendors selling their wares near expensive shops, women in brightly colored silk saris toting designer handbags, and men in Western-style suits walking past beggars on the street. In a nearly seamless blend of extremes, tradition and modernity, along with wealth and poverty, exist side by side. Everywhere you walk, you feel the energy of the people.

India's markets are crowded and bustling.

The mix of sounds, smells, and sights is awe inspiring and slightly dizzying. You decide to take a ride across the natural harbor to Elephanta Island. Only a short distance from the Gateway of India, Elephanta Island is home to ancient caves and beautiful sculptures and carvings. A visit to the holy site is just the break you need from the hustle of the modern city. On the way, a guide offers an informative introduction to Hinduism, the religion practiced by approximately 80 percent of Indians.

SACRED ARCHITECTURE

The caves of Elephanta Island were first carved into a natural temple between the sixth and eighth centuries CE. At the time, they were guarded by an impressive sculpture of an elephant carved from rock. The island was named for this sculpture by the Portuguese, who ruled India before the English. The stone elephant collapsed in 1814, and the pieces were reassembled in nearby Victoria Gardens.

The caves are dedicated to Shiva, the Hindu deity representing the cycle of destruction and creation. One of the treasures of Elephanta Island is a famous image of Sadashiva. This three-headed sculpture shows Shiva in his image of destroyer, Vishnu, the Hindu deity known as the preserver, and Brahma, the Hindu deity known as the creator.

As the day winds down, you board the boat back to Mumbai. Evening brings a relaxing stroll on the promenade along Chowpatty Beach. You join locals and visitors to watch the sunset and to enjoy the twinkling lights of nearby Marine Drive.

The caves at Elephanta Island feature ancient holy sites.

A MULTIDIMENSIONAL LAND

Vibrant, crowded, and multifaceted, Mumbai is representative of India as a whole. India is a land of extremes. Geographically, it is graced with lofty mountain peaks and dusty flatlands, tropical jungles and beautiful beaches. Financially, it is one of the world's fastest-growing economies, yet one-quarter of its citizens live in poverty. India is home to both the highest concentration of billionaires in Asia and one of the largest slums in Asia, where more than 1 million people live in extreme poverty.[1]

Nearly all of the world's major religions are practiced side by side in India. In Mumbai, shrines, mosques, and other places of worship are nestled among the shops, hotels, and homes. There, the famous Hindu Mahalaxmi Temple lies just a short distance from the Islamic Haji Ali Mosque, and the Jewish Knesseth Eliyahoo Synagogue is near the Christian Saint Thomas's Cathedral. Freedom of religion is a democratic right in India, and spirituality is an integral part of daily life for most Indians.

The crowds seen in Mumbai are present throughout India. Even though India is the second-most-populous nation in

NAME CHANGER

In 1995, the name of the city of Bombay was officially changed to Mumbai. "Bombay" is an Anglicized version of *Mumbai* and the city's original name. While many Indians still refer to the city as Bombay, speakers of two common local languages, Marathi and Gujarati, have always called it Mumbai.

The skyline of Mumbai lights up the night.

DHARAVI SLUM

The Dharavi slum is one of the largest slums in Asia. It is situated between two main railways in the financial district of Mumbai, India's industrial center. More than 1 million people live in its cramped huts amid open sewers and dirt-strewn lanes. To pay the extremely low rents charged in the Dharavi slum, many of the residents work at low-paying jobs or participate in one of the slum's thriving small industries, making garments, pottery, or leather goods for export. The government has plans to renovate the slum into a new township. Doing so will cost more than $2 billion and displace thousands of families.[2]

the world, it is only about one-third the geographic size of the United States. India's recent economic growth has been fueled by rapidly growing industry, but overcrowding remains one of the nation's challenges. The large population puts tremendous pressure on the environment and poses significant housing challenges.

In recent years, economists and journalists have referred to India as a future superpower. As India continues its rapid growth, it will grapple with how to include all of its many and diverse citizens in its booming economic development.

India is a complex and pluralistic society. Author Shashi Tharoor, who has written often and affectionately about his native India, wrote that defining the nation is nearly impossible. He asked, "How can one portray an ageless civilization that was the birthplace of four major religions, a dozen different traditions of classical dance, 85 political parties, and 300 ways of cooking the potato?"[3]

SNAPSHOT

Official name: Republic of India

Capital city: New Delhi

Form of government: federal republic

Title of leader: president

Currency: rupee

Population (July 2011 est.): 1,189,172,906
World rank: 2

Size: 1,268,884 square miles (3,287,263 sq km)
World rank: 7

Language: Hindi and English; government also recognizes 14 other official languages

Official religion: none (Unofficial religion: Hindu, 80.5% of population)

Per capita GDP (2010, US dollars): $3,400
World rank: 163

CHAPTER 2
GEOGRAPHY: A LAND OF VARIETY

Located in one of the most varied geographic regions on Earth, India boasts lofty peaks and flat plains, dry deserts and humid jungles, and twisting rivers and resplendent beaches. Much of the nation is a peninsula, surrounded by the Arabian Sea on the west and the Bay of Bengal on the east. India's landscape offers travelers numerous possibilities, including mountain treks, camelback desert tours, and visits to rain forests, rivers, coastlines, and island beaches.

In terms of geographic size, India is the second-largest nation in Asia and the seventh-largest nation in the world.[1] The Indian subcontinent is separated from the rest of Asia by the Himalayan Mountains. The subcontinent was formed approximately 40 million years ago when a chunk of the earth's crust was pushed against the continent of Asia.

The Himalayan Mountains include the tallest peaks in the world.

19

AVERAGE TEMPERATURE AND RAINFALL

Region (City)	Average January Temperature Minimum/ Maximum	Average July Temperature Minimum/Maximum	Average Rainfall January/July
Northern Mountains (Darjeeling)	36/46°F (2/8°C)	57/66°F (14/19°C)	0.51/31.41 inches (1.3/79.8 cm)
Northern Plains (Kolkata)	55/81°F (13/27°C)	79/90°F (26/32°C)	0.39/12.8 inches (1/32.5 cm)
Thar Desert (nearest city: Jacobabad, Pakistan)	45/73°F (7/23°C)	86/109°F (30/43°C)	0.2/0.91 inches (0.5/2.3 cm)
Deccan Plateau (Hyderabad)	61/84°F (16/29°C)	73/88°F (23/31°C)	0.31/5.98 inches (0.8/15.2 cm)
West Coast (Mumbai)	66/82°F (19/28°C)	77/84°F (25/29°C)	0.1/24.29 inches (0.25/61.7 cm)
Southeastern Coast (Chennai)	66/84°F (19/29°C)	79/97°F (26/36°C)	1.42/3.58 inches (3.6/9.1 cm)[2]

India is bordered on the south by water: the Arabian Sea on the southwest and the Bay of Bengal on the southeast. India's neighbors to the north are China, Bhutan, and Nepal, and Sri Lanka is approximately

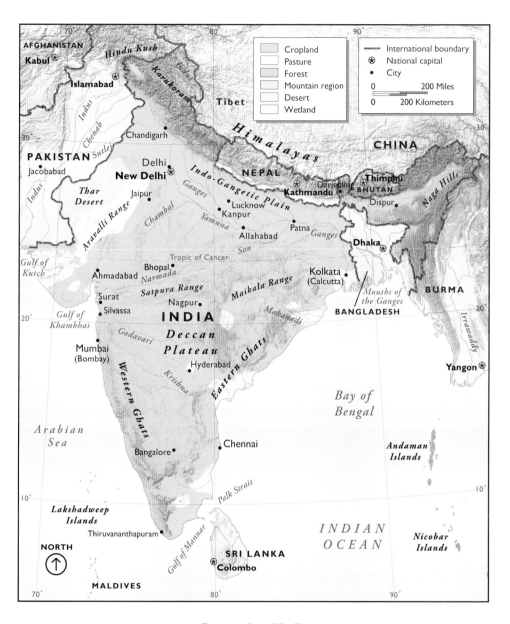

AFGHANISTAN
Kabul ⊛
Hindu Kush
Karakoram
Islamabad ⊛
Tibet

	Cropland
	Pasture
	Forest
	Mountain region
	Desert
	Wetland

- - -	International boundary
⊛	National capital
•	City

0 ——— 200 Miles
0 ——— 200 Kilometers

Indus
Chenab
Sutlej
Jhelum
Chandigarh •

H i m a l a y a s

CHINA

PAKISTAN
Jacobabad •
Delhi •
New Delhi ⊛
Indo-Gangetic Plain
NEPAL
Kathmandu ⊛
Darjeeling •
Thimphu ⊛
BHUTAN

Indus
Thar Desert
Jaipur •
Ganges
Lucknow •
Kanpur •
Allahabad •
Patna •
Ganges
Dispur •
Naga Hills

Aravalli Range
Chambal
Yamuna
Son
Dhaka ⊛

Gulf of Kutch
Tropic of Cancer
Ahmadabad •
Bhopal •
Narmada
Kolkata (Calcutta) •
Mouths of the Ganges
BURMA

Surat •
Silvassa •
Satpura Range
Nagpur •
Maikala Range
BANGLADESH
Irrawaddy

Gulf of Khambhai
INDIA
Godavari
Deccan Plateau
Mahanadi
Eastern Ghats

Mumbai (Bombay) •
Hyderabad •
Krishna

Arabian Sea
Western Ghats
Bangalore •
Chennai •
Bay of Bengal
Andaman Islands
Yangon ⊛

Palk Strait
Lakshadweep Islands
Thiruvananthapuram •
Gulf of Mannar
NORTH
↑
SRI LANKA
Colombo ⊛
I N D I A N O C E A N
Nicobar Islands

MALDIVES

Geography of India

one hour's boat ride to the south. To the northwest is Pakistan, and to the east are Burma and Bangladesh.

HOT, WET, AND COOL

India is considered to have three main seasons: hot, wet, and cool. The climate varies from north to south. The northern regions get very cold in the winter, and the southern regions get extremely hot in the summer.

India's varied climate can be divided into four primary zones. The alpine zone in the mountains endures heavy snowfalls and freezing temperatures. In the subtropical climate of much of northern India, the summer is quite hot with monsoon rains and the winter is quite cold. In the tropical zone of southern India, temperatures are high all year round, and rain is common. The western part of India is arid, with high temperatures and low rainfall.

The world's first cotton clothing was made in India.

The most temperate time to visit most parts of India is from November through February, when temperatures are cool. The hot season begins near the end of February, and it heats up considerably by May. The country can get extremely hot in the summer, and the northern mountains reach freezing temperatures in the winter.

The most prominent feature of India's climate is the monsoon season, which begins in the southern part of the

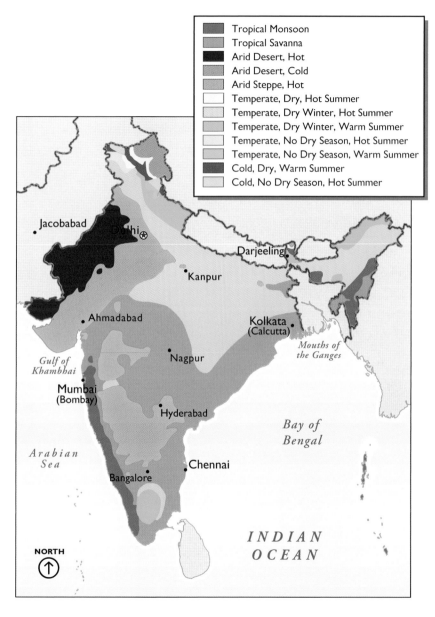

■	Tropical Monsoon
■	Tropical Savanna
■	Arid Desert, Hot
■	Arid Desert, Cold
■	Arid Steppe, Hot
□	Temperate, Dry, Hot Summer
▨	Temperate, Dry Winter, Hot Summer
▨	Temperate, Dry Winter, Warm Summer
□	Temperate, No Dry Season, Hot Summer
▨	Temperate, No Dry Season, Warm Summer
■	Cold, Dry, Warm Summer
□	Cold, No Dry Season, Hot Summer

Jacobabad

Delhi

Darjeeling

Kanpur

Ahmadabad

Kolkata
(Calcutta)

*Gulf of
Khambhai*

Nagpur

*Mouths of
the Ganges*

Mumbai
(Bombay)

Hyderabad

*Bay of
Bengal*

*Arabian
Sea*

Chennai

Bangalore

INDIAN
OCEAN

NORTH
↑

Climate of India

country in late May or early June and moves north to cover the majority of the country in hot, wet rain.

FROM THE MOUNTAINS TO THE SEA

India can be divided into three main geographic areas: the mountainous north, the fertile central plains, and the rocky southern plateau. But variations exist even within these regions, from hot deserts and steamy jungles to rocky peaks and sandy beaches. The Himalayas— the largest mountain range in the world—border northern India.

EARTHQUAKES AND MONSOONS

India is plagued by unstable land and weather. The country faces minor tremors and major earthquakes, as well as changeable amounts of rain in the annual monsoon season.

The dramatic geographic collision that formed India occurred millions of years ago, but the tectonic plates beneath the land remain active. As a result, India has experienced numerous earthquakes. In 1934, a devastating earthquake struck Bihar, killing more than 10,000 people. In 2001, an earthquake in the state of Gujarat killed 20,000 people and left another 500,000 without homes.[3]

India's geographic formation also created a particular wind system called the Indian monsoon. Instead of blowing in a single direction for most of the year, as is typical of the winds in most countries, the Indian monsoon changes directions. This wind brings India's heavy rains.

In 2005, increased rainfall caused flooding in Gujarat and Maharashtra, killing thousands of people. In September 2010, the rainfall was 44 percent above average during the monsoon season, resulting in devastating floods in the state of Uttar Pradesh that left millions of people homeless.[4]

The monsoon season can bring devastating floods to India.

The name *Himalaya* means "the abode of snow" in Sanskrit and is used to identify the mountain range that separates India from Tibet.[5] It is also used to refer to the cluster of mountain ranges nearby, including the Karakoram and the Hindu Kush. In India, these are divided into three areas: the Outer, the Lesser, and the Great Himalayas.

The Himalayas stretch approximately 1,550 miles (2,500 km) across India, southern Tibet, Nepal, and Bhutan.[6] The Himalayas are often referred to as "the roof of the world."[7] They are the highest mountains in the world, and they are still growing taller. The mountains' growth is due to the movement of the tectonic plates in the earth beneath them.

The Ganges River originates in the Himalayas and flows through the northern and central plains of India and into Bangladesh. From the Himalayas, the river flows southwest through the state of Uttarakhand and into a town called Haridwar, where a dam diverts the flow to the southeast.

A SACRED RIVER

The Ganges River is considered to be a holy place by Hindus, who worship the river as the goddess Ganga. The site where the Ganges meets the Yamuna River, in the city of Allahabad, is considered to be a particularly sacred spot.

The Ganges flows through flatlands that were once thick forests and are now densely populated and cultivated for agriculture. This area is called the Indo-Gangetic Plain. On the eastern coast are marshlands and tropical rain forests.

Many bathers consider the water of
the Ganges River to be holy.

To the west of the Indo-Gangetic Plain lies the vast Thar Desert, which spans northwestern India and eastern Pakistan. The Indian states of Rajasthan and Gujarat lie in this hot and dry desert land.

A ridge called the Deccan Plateau geographically divides northern and southern India. Scientists believe this plateau is the only visible portion of the ancient piece of land that formed the subcontinent. Two smaller mountain ranges called Ghats flank the plateau on either side. The Western Ghats drop into a coastal rain forest, and the Eastern Ghats are dissected by rivers that flow into the Bay of Bengal.

The Arabian Sea and the Bay of Bengal meet in the Indian Ocean at the southern tip of India. To the east lie the Andaman and Nicobar Islands. To the west are the Lakshadweep Islands, which have spectacular coral reefs.

India's diverse land is divided into 28 states and seven territories. The nation's capital, New Delhi, is in northern India, and its industrial center, Mumbai, is on the western coast in the state of Rajasthan.

Located in India's northeast, the state of Rajasthan is very arid.

CHAPTER 3

ANIMALS AND NATURE: RICH BIODIVERSITY

India's varied landscape and climate support a huge selection of plants. The different habitats sustain one of the most vibrant animal populations in the world. India is well known as the home of the elephant, the monkey, and the rhino, but it is the tiger, the national animal, that represents India. This black and gold cat lives in multiple habitats, including dry savannas and wet rain forests. The Bengal tiger, a tiger subspecies, is the most common tiger in India.

In the 1930s, scientists estimated that there were 40,000 tigers living in India. By 1972, when the first official census of tigers was taken, there were only 1,800 left.[1] This shocking finding prompted then–prime minister Indira Gandhi to make the tiger the official symbol of India and to launch Project Tiger, a comprehensive program to protect the animals. The project set up reserves to protect the tigers and all the animals and

The Bengal tiger is India's national animal.

SPIRITUAL AID FOR TIGERS

Decreasing tiger numbers is partially a result of the high demand for tiger skins and body parts in China and Tibet. In China, the tigers' bones and other body parts are used in ancient medicine. In Tibet, tiger pelts have been used in spiritual ceremonies and worn as a symbol of wealth for years. While the Chinese continue to buy and sell tiger parts, change has come to Tibet.

New Delhi–based conservationist Belinda Wright explained the problem to the spiritual and political leader of Tibet, the Dalai Lama. In January 2006, he spoke out in support of the tigers. Many Tibetans heard the Dalai Lama speak of the need to protect the tigers. After the speech, Tibetans burned tiger skins, giving a ceremonial message that the Dalai Lama's call had been heard and that they would stop buying and selling tiger skins and body parts. The news brought renewed hope to some conservationists.

Nonetheless, the market for tigers is still strong in China. Valmik Thapar, an Indian tiger expert, is not convinced the danger is over. "Even if the Tibetans have really stopped buying tiger skins . . . there is very little chance of the tiger surviving in India."[3]

plants in the tigers' natural habitat.

Since Project Tiger was founded, it has established 27 protective reserves in India. Initially, the government program was successful in limiting the poaching, or killing, of tigers. But recently, the number of tigers in India has dropped further to 1,400.[2] Tigers continue to face extinction in India and all over the world.

ANIMALS IN INDIA

From the largest mammals, including Bengal tigers and Indian elephants, to tiny birds called sunbirds, by

Many species of sunbirds live in India.

one count, India has 397 species of mammals, 1,232 types of birds, and thousands of unique species of insects and fish.[4] Among India's animal population are a number of rare animals, including the snow leopard, the red panda, the one-horned rhinoceros, and the Ganges river dolphin. In addition, India is the only nation in the world where both lions and tigers live.

Some animals live throughout the nation of India, including the large and much-loved Indian elephants and a wide variety of snakes and primates. However, other animals are found only in particular habitats within India's varied regions. For example, the cold peaks and low-lying foothills of the Himalayas provide homes for hardy animals that can withstand the weather. Yaks and two-humped camels, domesticated by the villagers in the foothills, thrive in this area. The Himalayan tahr, or mountain goat, and the bharal, or blue sheep, also live in this area. Rare and threatened species of the Himalayas include the Tibetan antelope and the musk deer.

HOLY ANIMALS

Many animals are sacred to Hindus. The cow, in particular, has been considered holy for centuries and is protected throughout India. Hindus also revere the elephant, considered an incarnation of the Hindu deity Ganesh. The elephant is the official animal of the state of Kerala and is a common site at temples and in sacred ceremonies in southwestern India.

The yak is adapted to cold and mountainous regions.

The desert to the southwest of the Himalayas, in the states of Rajasthan and Gujarat, is home to creatures that thrive in the hot, dry conditions. Among the animals that live there are chinkaras, or Indian gazelle; blackbucks, a large breed of antelope; Indian wolves; and an array of wild dogs, hyenas, and deer. A sanctuary in the desert of Gujarat is also the last refuge of the once-common Asiatic lion.

The Asiatic lion is the only lion subspecies still living outside of Africa.

The tropical forests of the Western Ghats in southern India provide a home for an impressive variety of birds and other animals. Leopards, sloth bears, jungle cats, and flying lizards live in these forests alongside hundreds of birds, including parrots and hornbills. Rare animals in this area include the small Salim Ali's fruit bat and the Nilgiri tahr, or cloud goat, an endangered animal that lives in the hills.

The islands off the shore of India provide a home for a variety of fish and marine life. Bottlenose dolphins, sea turtles, and tropical fish swim among the large coral ecosystems. Elephants living in the Andaman Islands swim between islands. Butterflies and seabirds also thrive in the lush climate of the islands.

India is also home to both rare and common primates. One of the most common is the rhesus macaque, a stocky, pink-faced monkey seen

Langur monkeys sit in the ruins of a fort in Rajasthan.

INDIAN SNAKES

India has nearly 400 species of snakes, and about one in five of these snakes is venomous.[6] The king cobra, one of the most common forms of venomous snakes, can grow up to 12 feet (3.7 m) long. Nonvenomous snakes include the rock python and a bright green snake called the vine snake.

A mammal called the snake-killing mongoose preys on India's snakes. The crafty hunter tricks the snake into striking it over and over to the point of exhaustion. Then the mongoose attacks, eating the snake's head first to avoid a deadly snakebite.

all over India. Rare primates include the long-armed hoolock gibbon and the furry golden langur in the northeast.

PLANTS IN INDIA

By one count, India has 49,219 species of plants, 5,200 of which are endemic, or live only in one location.[5] The plants vary by region. At one time, India was almost entirely covered in forests, but because of destructive agricultural practices, India's forest is now estimated to cover approximately one-quarter of the nation.

Different types of forests exist throughout India. Coniferous forests are found in the Himalayas, where blue pine and Himalayan cedar grow. The rain forests of the Western Ghats, which are populated with evergreen trees, remain lush throughout the year. But other types of

Teak wood is valuable because it is strong and can last for centuries.

ENDANGERED SPECIES IN INDIA

According to the International Union for Conservation of Nature (IUCN), India is home to the following numbers of species that are categorized by the organization as Critically Endangered, Endangered, or Vulnerable:

Mammals	94
Birds	78
Reptiles	30
Amphibians	66
Fishes	122
Mollusks	2
Other Invertebrates	111
Plants	255
Total	758[7]

trees have been largely cleared from these forests, including Indian rosewood, Malabar kino, and teak. Deciduous forests—with sal, teak, mango, bamboo, and rosewood trees— grow on the western and northeastern sides of the Deccan Plateau in northern India and in the lower ranges of the Himalayas.

Throughout northern India, except the northeast, grow dry deciduous forests. These include teak, sal, sandalwood, mahua, khair, mango, jackfruit, wattle, bamboo, and banyan trees. Bamboos, ferns, and grasses grow in the northern mountains and foothills, and the khejri tree and scrub acacias grow in the arid desert. More than 100 species of palm trees grow in the tropical south and on the islands, along with coconut and betel nut trees. Trees that are common throughout India include mango trees, with delicious fruit, and two types of ficus trees: the papal and the banyan.

ENVIRONMENTAL THREATS AND SOLUTIONS

India faces numerous threats to its rich natural environment. The same development of industry that has fueled the nation's economic growth has been devastating to its environment. Approximately 65 percent of India's land has been degraded in some way since the use of chemical fertilizers became common in India in the 1960s.[8] Deforestation, or the removal of forests, destroys the natural habitats of India's plants and animals.

India's rapidly growing population also poses a threat to the vulnerable environment. Natural areas are sacrificed as urban centers expand to accommodate the country's more than 1 billion citizens. And as these large, heavily populated areas grow, air, water, and noise pollution

VALLEY OF FLOWERS

The best place to see many of India's thousands of species of flowering plants is the Valley of Flowers National Park in the state of Uttarakhand in the northwest. There, approximately 300 species of wildflowers grow in their natural habitat, creating waves of color across the gentle slopes of the Himalayan foothills.[9] The Valley of Flowers is one of India's 28 World Heritage sites chosen by the United Nations Educational, Scientific, and Cultural Organization (UNESCO).

India has 503 endangered, threatened, or vulnerable species of animals.

wreak havoc on the environment and pose serious health concerns, including respiratory diseases and limited access to clean water.

In response to severe environmental damage, the Indian government has set aside large tracts of land for protection and conservation. India's first national park, now known as Corbett National Park, was established in 1935. Today, nature is protected in 99 national parks and 513 wildlife sanctuaries.[10] Fifteen areas called biosphere reserves overlap different parks, creating safe channels for animals and birds to travel and migrate.[11]

India's national parks protect many species, including Indian rhinoceroses such as this one in Kaziranga National Park in Assam.

CHAPTER 4
HISTORY: AN EPIC PAST

India's history stretches back at least 4,000 centuries. Axes and other artifacts of human civilization found in the area that is now Rajasthan date back at least 400,000 years.

India's early peoples lived in nomadic tribes. They thrived primarily in the area called the Indus valley, around the Indus River. People believed to be indigenous to India are called Dravidian. Tools, weapons, rock paintings, and carvings found in the Indus valley indicate that a factory center was established in the area between 140,000 and 25,000 years ago. Similar evidence shows the first permanent settlement was established further inland about 9,000 years ago in the area that is now Madhya Pradesh.

Bust of a priest-king from Mohenjo-daro

As time passed, the tribes became more settled in the fertile Indus valley. By approximately 5100 BCE, the people had begun to harvest an early form of wheat. The region's first urban centers, Harappa and Mohenjo-daro, located in modern Pakistan, flourished in the third and second millennia BCE.

The game of chess was invented in India.

These cities marked the beginning of India's first major urban civilization, the Indus valley civilization. Also called the Harappan civilization, this culture thrived for approximately 1,000 years. The Harappans created art with terracotta and bronze, invented a system of weights and measures, and made figures thought to be early forms of Hindu deities.

WAVES OF CIVILIZATIONS

Scholars dispute how and why the Harappan civilization ended and what marked the beginning of the next major civilization in India, the Vedic period of the Aryan civilization. Some scholars believe that the water dried up in the Indus valley, forcing the Harappan people to leave. Some contend that the Dravidians left after the Aryans came from Afghanistan and central Asia and invaded the valley, while others believe that the Aryans did not invade the region but rather gradually pushed the Dravidians further south. A less fully developed theory holds that the Aryans were also native to India.

The Aryans in India wrote the Vedas, a body of sacred writings that formed the foundations of Hinduism. The civilization they founded—the Vedic civilization—thrived between 1500 and 500 BCE. India's caste system, by which society is organized by classes of individuals, also is believed to have been formed during this time. In 500 BCE, India became the birthplace of two more of the world's religions: Buddhism and Jainism.

The Vedic people began as a group of tribes that herded livestock and later developed agriculture. They later organized themselves into 16 kingdoms, which eventually fused into four large states. From these states arose the Nanda dynasty, or ruling family, which controlled much of northern India from approximately 364 BCE. During the Nanda dynasty, India avoided two serious invasions.

In 321 BCE, a leader named Chandragupta Maurya wrested control from the Nanda dynasty and founded the first major Indian empire. Under this leader, all of India was united under one government for the first time. The well-organized and highly structured Maurya Empire reached its peak with the emperor Ashoka. When he died in 232 BCE, the empire began to crumble, eventually falling in 185 BCE.

SACRED STORIES

The *Ramayana* and the *Mahabharata* are stories about the heroes Rama and Krishna that became important Hindu texts. These tales were first told in the Vedic civilization and then handed down orally from one generation to the next. They were only later written down.

For a time, smaller tribes and kingdoms controlled individual realms of India. But in 320 CE, a king named Chandra Gupta I amassed power to found the next great Indian empire. The Gupta Empire grew over the years, passing leadership down through the family line. The arts, literature, and poetry flourished, and Hinduism became the dominant religion. This time period became known as India's Golden Age. But this enlightened empire fell due to an invasion by the Huns, a nomadic central Asian group, in approximately 510 CE.

After the fall of the Gupta Empire, northern and southern India developed separately for a time. The South developed as a primarily Hindu region, and the North was organized into what were predominantly Islamic tribes. During this time, in 1498, the first European came to India: a Portuguese sailor named Vasco da Gama. Not long

ELLORA CAVES

The Ellora Caves in Maharashtra feature religious art and carvings dating back to 600 CE. This UNESCO World Heritage site includes the work of three religions, Hinduism, Buddhism, and Jainism, spread among 34 caves. The caves served as a monastery and temple complex for four centuries, with caves belonging to each of the three religions being created and occupied at the same time. The site is a vivid example of the spirit of religious harmony that flourished in India at the time.

The Ellora Caves in Maharashtra feature buildings and sculptures dating from 600 to 1000 CE, honoring Hinduism, Buddhism, and Jainism.

Late sixteenth-century Mughal court scene

afterward, in 1510, Portuguese traders fought the sultan, Yusuf Adil Khan, for control of Goa. Initially defeated, the Europeans tried again after the sultan's death and were victorious. The Portuguese took control of the small region of Goa, giving them access to the region's trade goods.

Despite this defeat in Goa, the Mughal Empire rose to prominence throughout India during this time, beginning under Babur in 1526. The empire remained in power through the 1700s. The arts and architecture flourished under the Mughals, who were Islamic. But Indians of the Hindu faith fought back for power and territory. In particular, two groups fought the Mughals: the Rajputs and the Marathas.

COLONIZATION

As groups of Indians fought for power, more foreigners began to arrive on the subcontinent. Queen Elizabeth I of England authorized the first trade mission to India in 1600. A year later, the British East India Company arrived and set up a trading post. For the next 150 years, the British traded in India. By the 1700s, they wanted more control over the region. By this time, the French had also arrived, claiming Pondicherry (today called Puducherry) in southern India in 1674. For approximately 100 years, the French and the British competed for control of areas of India.

When Aurangzeb, the last great Mughal leader, died in 1707, Islamic rule over regions of India was severely compromised. His death coincided with a time of increasingly powerful Hindu uprisings and the frequent arrival of European traders.

At the start of the nineteenth century, India was ruled by a series of maharajas, or princes. But British power had expanded so much that areas of

HINDU WARRIORS

As the Mughal Empire grew, two groups fought against its rule. The Rajputs of Rajasthan were famous warriors. They bravely fended off Mughal rule until infighting between them caused their states to be defeated and absorbed into the Mughal Empire. Another group, the Marathas, who were also Hindus, were more successful in fighting off the Mughals for a time. Their success was largely due to a warrior named Shivaji. Tales of Shivaji's heroics in and around the area of the region of Maharashtra between the years 1646 and 1680 are still told in India. Shivaji established the Maratha kingdom in western India and beyond. It thrived until Afghan forces defeated the Marathas in 1761.

BLACK HAWK MIDDLE SCHOOL
EAGAN, MN

An artist's representation of the British receiving rent
from Indian rulers, late eighteenth century

India had come under British political control. Opposed to British rule of their lands, Indian soldiers rebelled in 1857 in what is known as the First War of Independence.

After the British victory over the Indian rebellion in 1858, the monarchy took control from the East India Trading Company, establishing what became known as the British Raj, or rule, throughout India. English became the official language, and a British viceroy, or supervisor, was appointed to rule over India.

Indians responded by forming a political party, the Indian National Congress, in 1885. Members of Congress, as the party is still known,

THE INDIAN UPRISING

By the mid-nineteenth century, the British had established economic, political, and cultural control over much of India. In some cases, they took power directly from Indian rulers. Cheap British goods took the place of Indian-made products in local markets, causing craftspeople to lose their incomes. The British also imposed strict taxes on landowning Indians. Indian dissatisfaction came to a head on May 10, 1857, in a battle that has become known as the Indian Mutiny or the First War of Independence.

A rumor circulated about a new type of bullet being dipped in cow fat or pig fat. To use these bullets, a soldier was required to bite off the greased portion. Because the cow is sacred to Hindus and Muslims do not consume pig products, the new bullets were deeply offensive to Indian soldiers of both religions. The use of these bullets appeared to be symbolic of British rule over India.

A British officer forced the men to bite off the ends of their bullets. When outraged Indian soldiers refused, they were imprisoned. Quickly, the prisoners joined with local peasants to fight against British rule. Indians held power for some months in the areas of Delhi and Lucknow but were then defeated by the British.

lobbied for greater participation in government. Eventually, some were appointed as councillors to the English viceroy. Many Indians opposed British rule, however. In 1905, they participated in widespread protests when Great Britain attempted to partition off Bengal, a region of India.

INDEPENDENCE

As the British Raj imposed increasingly steep tariffs and passed laws considered to be unfair to many Indians, more and more Indians opposed British rule. An Indian lawyer and member of the Congress Party, Mohandas Gandhi, emerged as a leader of the movement for independence.

Gandhi taught a committed form of nonviolent civil disobedience, in which unfair laws and conditions are protested without the use of weapons or destruction. For example, in the early 1900s, Gandhi promoted a national strike against a new law that allowed the British to imprison Indians without trial under certain circumstances. Indians responded with what were largely peaceful protests all over the country.

However, a protest on April 13, 1919, in Amritsar in the state of Punjab met a deadly attack by armed British soldiers. More than 5,000 protesters, including many women and children, had gathered in a walled-in area called Jallianwallah Bagh to express their discontent with the law. When British soldiers, led by Brigadier-General Reginald Dyer, entered the area, they fired on the protesters, killing an estimated 1,500 people.[1]

Gandhi, appalled and saddened, called off the national strike in the aftermath of the massacre.

But Gandhi continued to support and promote civil disobedience. In 1942, he launched the nonviolent Quit India campaign, calling for an immediate end to British rule in India. Of the movement, Gandhi stated, "We shall either free India or die in the attempt; we shall not live to see the perpetuation of our slavery."[2]

After more bloodshed and struggle, India won independence on August 15, 1947.

The second half of the twentieth century was a time of tremendous growth and change for India, but it

MAHATMA GANDHI

Mohandas Gandhi was born in the state of Gujarat in India on October 2, 1869. He studied law in England and worked in South Africa as a young lawyer. Upon returning home in 1915, Gandhi became a leader in the fight for Indian independence. His followers called him *Mahatma*, which means "great soul."

Gandhi's leadership was courageous, steadfast, and ingenious. In 1930, in response to a British-imposed tax on salt, he led a massive march in Gujarat to the coast. There, he evaporated seawater to make salt, demonstrating that Indians could refuse to purchase the taxed salt and instead make their own.

Gandhi was committed to the principle of *ahimsa*, a Sanskrit word and Hindu doctrine that means "nonviolence" or "not causing harm to others." He believed in a tolerant, united India and played a major role in the nation's fight for independence. Gandhi also opposed separating India into Hindu and Muslim states, which met with discontent from some religious extremists.

On January 30, 1948, shortly after India had gained its independence from the United Kingdom, Gandhi was going to a prayer meeting when a Hindu nationalist killed him. Gandhi was a symbol of courage, peace, and steadfast commitment. His death was mourned the world over.

Mohandas Gandhi's nonviolent leadership helped win India's independence.

was marked by periods of civil and religious unrest. One family led the nation for several decades, beginning with the first prime minister, Jawarhalal Nehru. The popular leader led the nation through its jubilant early years of independence and initiated a Five-Year Plan to promote prosperity and unity. Nehru died in 1964 and was succeeded by a member of his cabinet, Lal Bahadur Shastri, until Shastri died in 1966. Nehru's daughter, Indira Gandhi, then became prime minister. She saw the nation through a territorial war with Pakistan, a traumatic recession, and a time in which increasing religious differences led to civil unrest. This came to a head in 1984 when she was assassinated by one of her bodyguards, a Sikh separatist. But the Nehru line continued when Gandhi's son, Rajiv Gandhi, succeeded her as prime minister. Rajiv Gandhi's political party lost power in 1989 and he was forced to leave office. In 1991, he was assassinated while running for prime minister a second time.

Tensions between religious groups in India continued through the twentieth century and into the twenty-first, and India has suffered from terrorist attacks, including a devastating three-day attack in 2008. Deadly earthquakes shook the country in 2001 and 2005. But none of these challenges could stop India from developing its economy, thanks in large part to a technology boom. This was fueled by India's talented engineers and scientists as well as by hardworking Indians who moved to urban areas to work in calls centers. Technology and other industries continue to transform the Indian economy, lifting many but certainly not all of the nation's citizens out of poverty and causing economists to predict that India will become a new global economic superpower.

Mohandas Gandhi first confronted racial issues in South Africa in the 1890s.

CHAPTER 5
PEOPLE: DIVERSE YET UNITED

The diversity among India's tribes and clans, communities and cities, religious and cultural affiliations, and most of all, its many languages rivals the diversity of its geography. From north to south and east to west, India is a land of contradictions and extremes. But among these differences lives a common people.

In his book about India's history, author Shashi Tharoor observed:

What makes so many people one people? One answer is the physical realities of the subcontinent—mountains to the north and northwest, water surrounding the rest—which have carved out a distinct geographical space for Indians to inhabit....A second, equally revealing, answer may be found in the attitude of generations of foreigners, from Alexander the Great to the first of the Great

Members of a nomadic tribe from India's arid western region

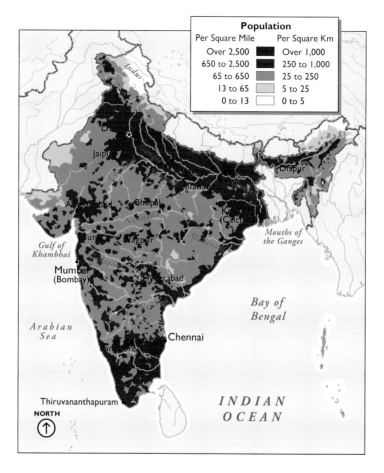

Population Density of India

Mughals, Babur, who consistently saw the peoples of the land beyond the Indus—"Hindustan"—as one. Divided, variegated, richly differentiated, but one.[1]

One of many differences among Indians is language. The primary languages of the country are Hindi and, for official documents, English, but each state also has its own language. For example, the state language of Kerala is Malayalam, and the state language of Karnataka is Kannada. Even though more people in India speak Hindi than any other language, only 41 percent of Indians speak Hindi.[2]

LANGUAGE AND MEANING

The Hindi language communicates something about the Indian mindset. For example, the word for hello, *namaste*, also means good-bye, and the word for tomorrow, *kal*, also means yesterday. Time in India is understood as a process or as part of an ongoing cycle. So the end, or *good-bye*, is already present in the beginning, the *hello*, and the past, *yesterday*, is evident in the future, *tomorrow*, and vice versa.

In addition to Hindi and English, the national constitution recognizes 14 more official languages: Bengali, Telugu, Marathi, Tamil, Urdu, Gujarati, Malayalam, Kannada, Oriya, Punjabi, Assamese, Kashmiri, Sindhi, and Sanskrit.

The Indian languages are derived from Indo-European and Dravidian roots. Historically, there were two main language groups: the Indo-Aryan Prakrit in the north and the Dravidian Tamil in the south. Sanskrit, another early Indo-Aryan language that developed in the Vedic period, remains the sacred language of Hindu texts.

YOU SAY IT!

English	Hindi	Bengali	Tamil
Hello	Namaste (nah-mah-STEH)	Muslim: Asalaam alaykum (ahs-SAH-lahm wah-LAY-koom) Hindu: Nomaashkaar (NOH-mohsh-kahr)	Vanakkam (vuh-nuhk-koom)
Good-bye	Namaste (nah-mah-STEH)	Muslim: Allah hafiz (AHL-lah HAH-fehz) Hindu: Nomaashkaar (NOH-mohsh-kahr)	Poyittu varukiren (pow-yiht-too vuh-roo-kih-rehn)
Excuse me	Kshamaa keejiye (k'shuh-mah KEE-jih-yee)	Shunum (SHOO-noom)	Mannikkavum (muh-nihk-kuh-voom)
Thank you	Danyavaad (duhn-yuh-vahd)	Dhnnobad (doh-noh-bahd)	Nanri (nuhn-rih)

Women sort red peppers for sale. A majority of Indians work in agricultural jobs.

Young Buddhist monks from India's northern mountains

PEOPLE OF INDIA

With more than 1 billion people, India is the second-most-populous nation on Earth. Just over half of Indians work in agriculture. Many of them are farmers who live in the fertile area of the Indo-Gangetic Plain, the most populated area of India. Others live in the south of India. Approximately one-third of India's people live in the nation's bustling cities.[3]

The majority of Indian people come from either Indo-Aryan or Dravidian ancestry. Seventy-two percent of Indians are of Indo-Aryan heritage, and 25 percent are Dravidian. Another 3 percent are of Mongoloid ancestry, with roots in Russia and China.[4]

Distinct physical characteristics, languages, customs, and religions distinguish Indians in different parts of the country. Indo-Aryans in the northern Indian states of Rajasthan, Punjab, and Delhi tend to be taller and have fairer skin than those living in the more centralized states of Uttar Pradesh and Madhya Pradesh. Indians living in the eastern states—including Assam, Manipur, Nagaland, and Mizoram—tend to be native Dravidian or Mongolian. Physically and culturally, they have much in common with their neighbors to the east in Burma and Nepal.

LANGUAGES IN INDIA

Language	Indians Who Speak the Language (in percent)
Hindi	41%
Bengali	8.1%
Telugu	7.2%
Marathi	7%
Tamil	5.9%
Urdu	5%
Gujarati	4.5%
Kannada	3.7%
Malayalam	3.2%
Oriya	3.2%
Punjabi	2.8%
Assamese	1.3%
Maithili	1.2%
Other languages	5.9%[5]

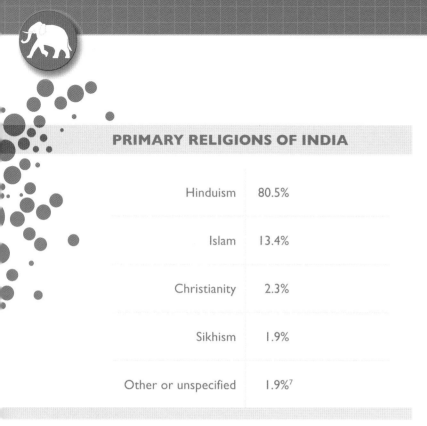

PRIMARY RELIGIONS OF INDIA

Hinduism	80.5%
Islam	13.4%
Christianity	2.3%
Sikhism	1.9%
Other or unspecified	1.9%[7]

Overall, India is a young country, with an average age of 26.2 years. The majority of Indians, 64.9 percent, are between the ages of 15 and 64. Children up to the age of 14 make up another 29.7 percent of the population, and only 5.5 percent of Indians are age 65 or older. The average life expectancy for Indians is 66.8 years old. Women live slightly longer, to approximately 67.95 years, and men slightly shorter, to 65.77 years.[6]

RELIGION AND DAILY LIFE

India is a secular country, and freedom of religion is a democratic right. Two of the world's most widely practiced religions, Hinduism and

Women of the Bonda tribe in Orissa. The Bonda tribe preserves its ancient customs and speaks a language unlike its neighbors.

Buddhism, were founded in India and are still practiced there today, alongside nearly every religion in the world.

Religion is deeply embedded in daily life. Shopkeepers offer prayers to the gods before starting business, and altars are commonplace in Indian homes.

More than 80 percent of Indians are Hindu, and this religion has a significant place in both India's history and in its modern lifestyle. Images of the colorful pantheon of Hindu deities are evident in temples as well as billboards and advertisements, and devotional rituals such as bathing in the Ganges River and performing *puja*, or prayers, are common.

SIKHISM

Sikhism emerged in the early sixteenth century in the Punjab region. Its followers believe in a single god. They believe in equality, sharing, and the pursuit of truth. They strive to avoid lust, anger, greed, and pride in order to achieve salvation. The tenets of Sikhism were shared by ten gurus, or teachers, who lived between the sixteenth and seventeenth centuries. Sikhism is similar to Hinduism in its belief in karma and reincarnation. However, Sikhism is against the worship of any images or statues and does not have priests.

A by-product of Hinduism that influenced India's people for centuries was a social institution known as the caste system. This hierarchic social structure designated a person's class and occupation from birth. This ensured radically different life experiences based on caste even for people of similar religious and ethnic backgrounds.

The caste system originated in the Vedic civilization and remained in place until its gradual devolution in the mid-twentieth century. The four main castes were the Brahmins (who were priests and scholars), followed by the Kshatriyas (soldiers), the Vaishyas (merchants), and the Sudras (laborers). Each caste was then subdivided into many different levels and types. Beneath all the castes was a group called the Dalits, referred to as untouchables, who were considered unclean and were often shunned by society.

Although the caste system is no longer officially

HINDUISM

Hinduism is one of the world's oldest religions. It is the predominant religion in India, where it began in approximately 500 BCE. Unlike most religions, Hinduism does not have a founder or a prophet or a single scripture or path to goodness or salvation. Instead, it offers followers a variety of paths and suggestions for proceeding through life in a righteous way. Many Hindus believe in reincarnation, that a person dies and is reborn repeatedly in different lives. Karma, or the balance of good and bad deeds in one's life, determines into what form the person is born in his or her next life.

Hinduism has many colorful deities, each of which is explained through stories and images. But Hindus believe that all deities are incarnations of one supreme God, or Brahma. Hinduism, as a whole, accepts all paths to the divine, meaning that it accepts as valid all the various understandings of God found in different religions.

Hindu values include tolerance, nonviolence, and right action. Right actions include devotion to the gods and participation in the different phases of life—from childhood to student life and family life to old age—with recommendations for right action in each phase.

recognized in India, caste consciousness persists in some regions and plays a role in many marriages. Even so, the Indian government has made a significant effort to undo the caste system and to open up opportunities to the historically underprivileged Dalits—for instance, reserving a number of places in universities and a percentage of government jobs for people of this caste.

RELIGIOUS CONFLICTS

Despite the Indian government's right to freedom of religion and people's general acceptance and embracing of spiritual differences, religion has also been a source of conflict, most commonly in clashes between Hindus and Muslims. One example is seen in the centuries-long conflict over the Babri Mosque in the northern city of Ayodhya.

The Babri Mosque was built by Babur, India's first Mughal ruler. It is located on land considered sacred by Hindus, where Ram, a Hindu deity, was born. In 1947, a group of conservative Hindus filed a court petition demanding rights to the land. After many years of relatively peaceful coexistence between Hindus and Muslims and acceptance of the mosque at this site, a group of Hindu nationalists destroyed it in 1992.

Colorful statues of the Hindu god Ganesh adorn a temple.

CHAPTER 6

CULTURE:
A COLORFUL NATION

Mountains shelter India's northern border, and water surrounds the rest of the nation. Viewed as a safe haven, India has drawn many settlers and colonizers over the years. More significantly, the nation's geography has supported development of a unique culture. India's lively culture is influenced by its thousands of years of history, the devotional character of its people, and its abiding sense of tolerance and embrace of difference.

In both small villages and large cities, color and crowds are two prominent features of Indian street life. The crowds come from the nation's large population, and color bursts from traditional clothing, images of deities, piles of spices, and more.

Festivals are a prominent feature of life in India. With such a devout culture and so many religions practiced, nearly every day of the year

In Jaipur, the Gangaur Festival is celebrated with dancing and processions.

sponsors a festival somewhere in India. Festivals are multiday events that traditionally begin with fasting and end with feasting. They vary, depending on the event and the region, but often include games, brightly colored decorations, flowers, and religious rituals.

FESTIVAL OF LIGHTS

One of the biggest festivals in India is Dewali, a Hindu celebration of light over darkness or sweetness over evil. The starting date of the festival varies each year, as it is determined by the position of the moon. The festival falls in the month of October or November and lasts for five days, with the third day being the most significant. Dewali celebrations include fireworks, games, decorations, special foods, and gift giving. The lighting of the *diya*, a clay lamp used for devotional purposes, is another important part of Dewali, as is the performing of daily *puja*, or prayers, to Lakshmi, the Hindu goddess of wealth. Dewali is celebrated in many Indian states, from north to south and east to west.

A FEAST FOR THE SENSES

Indian food is colorful, diverse, and aromatic. Food varies all across the country, and specialty dishes are native to each region. However, a typical Indian meal includes rice, lentils, vegetables, naan or roti (bread), and sometimes meat. India is famous for its spices—including cardamom from Kerala and saffron

Indian food features many colorful spices.

from Kashmir—and spices punctuate curries soups, and a variety of vegetable dishes.

Well-known Indian foods include a variety of vegetarian dishes, such as *kaalan*, a yogurt curry, and *sambar*, a lentil stew, which are common in the south. Tandoori chicken is made in a clay oven and comes from Punjab. Dal, a form of curried lentils, is enjoyed all over India and comes in many varieties.

Indians typically eat a light breakfast and lunch and enjoy a more substantial dinner. *Nashta*, or breakfast, may consist of stuffed flatbreads called *parathas* or a spongy rice cake called *idli*. Lentils are common to many Indian dishes and may be prepared as a soup called *sambar* for breakfast. Lunch varies and can include a *thali*, or selection of dishes, or *dosas*, flat pancake-like breads stuffed with potatoes, meat, or vegetables. Indians typically eat dinner as a family later in the evening, about 9:00 p.m. A variety of dishes are served with rice or roti and finished with fruit.

Colorful and sticky, Indian sweets tend to be reserved for celebrations and festivals. But a sweet tooth can be satisfied daily with chai, a tea made with milk and sugar. Also popular are soft drinks, fruit juice, and *lassi*, a drink made with yogurt.

Traditionally, Indian meals are eaten without utensils.

Naan served with a lentil dish

HEALING MIND, BODY, AND SPIRIT

Ayurveda is a system of health derived from ancient India. It is cited in the Vedas, the body of sacred writings developed by the Vedic civilization between 1500 and 500 BCE.

Ayurveda considers health a balance of systems integrating the mind, the body, and the soul or spirit. Ayurveda holds that everything is composed of the elements of space, air, fire, water, and earth. Health consists of balancing these elements, so a healthy individual is also in balance with a harmonious environment. Ayurveda defines three primary constitutions: *vata*, *pitta*, and *kapha*. Each is understood to be naturally inclined toward one element: air, fire, or water. Individuals are treated based on their unique constitutions.

The principles of this ancient system influence Indian approaches to food, health, and beauty. Modern medicine is widespread and highly developed in India, but some people still partake in ayurvedic treatments, which include herbs, specialized diets, massage, and hair and skin oils.

The interrelationship between daily life and spiritual pursuits that is so evident in India permeates diet, too. Specific rules apply to different religions. For instance, Muslims avoid pork products, and Hindus do not eat beef. Among Hindus, food is generally understood as related to spiritual and physical health. Vegetarianism is common in respect to the doctrine of ahimsa, or nonharm, and in keeping with ayurveda, a traditional Indian system of health and well-being. Devout Hindus do not drink alcohol or eat onions and garlic, which are believed to arouse sexual energy and create imbalances.

EXERCISING MIND AND BODY

Leisure and exercise in India include traditional and modern games and sports. In villages, children play games such as hopscotch and a game called Five Stones, tossing stones in the air and catching them in various patterns.

In some schools, children learn yoga, a form of physical and mental exercise native to India. Many adults also practice yoga for mental, physical, and spiritual health, and India's renowned yoga schools and teachers attract students from all over the world.

One of the nation's most popular pastimes, cricket, came from England. It is played with a bat and a ball, and in some ways is similar to baseball. Cricket teams attract big sponsors, and the athletes become national celebrities. Maharajah Ranjitsinhji Vibhaji was a renowned cricketer in the 1800s and early 1900s, and batsman Sachin Tendulkar is one of the best in the world today. In 2011, India won the Cricket World Cup. Other sports are also popular, including tennis, polo, hockey, and soccer.

ART AND ARCHITECTURE

Arts and crafts are integral to daily life in India. Traditional and modern art thrive side by side, including everything from delicate, hand-painted symbols on bodies and doorways to contemporary abstract paintings,

from the world's earliest clay sculptures to larger-than-life piles of shiny metal tins that fetch high prices at international auctions.

Indian arts have played a pivotal role in art history, from their origins up through the present day. Cave paintings made more than 55,500 years ago have been found in Bhimbetka. Successive residents of the Indus valley made sculptures from clay, bronze, and stone that are still admired by art historians. Particularly renowned are pink sandstone sculptures made during the Gupta period and intricate miniature paintings made during the seventeenth century in Rajasthan.

More recently, Indian artists have become important figures in contemporary art, often infusing their work with elements of Indian culture. S. H. Raza, a well-known Indian painter living in France, references the *bindi*, a dot representing a central point of knowledge or gateway to wisdom, alongside abstract shapes. Subodh Gupta, a

PAINTINGS FOR GODS BIG AND SMALL

Colorful patterns and designs painted on doorsteps are common in many parts of India. These handmade pictures, called *rangoli*, are a Hindu tradition designed to honor or welcome the deities into one's home. They are made of colored rice powder, which is edible to insects, so prayer is beneficial to even the tiniest creatures.

The Lakshmana Temple in Madhya Pradesh is part of a UNESCO World Heritage site today.

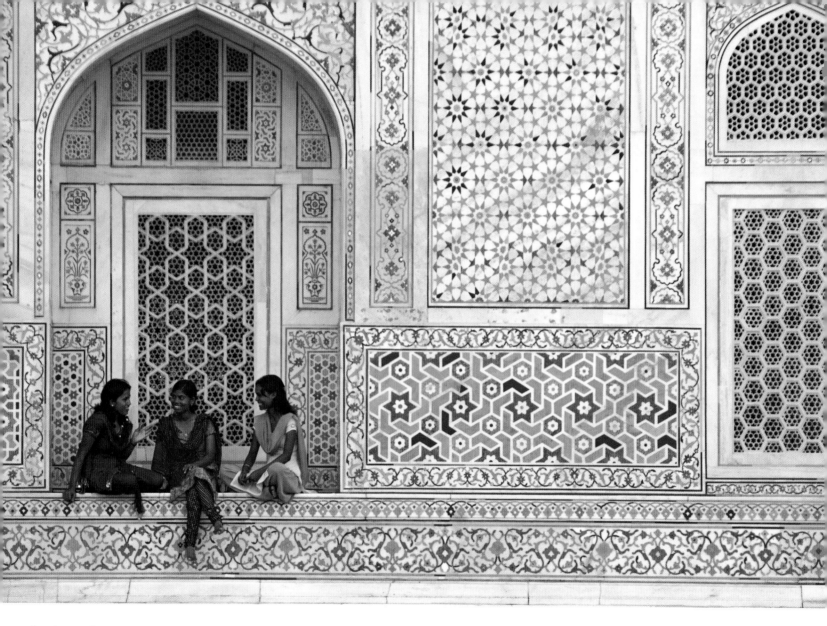

Intricate abstract patterns decorate a Mughal
tomb in Uttar Pradesh.

contemporary sculptor, uses commonplace Indian items, such as an Indian lunchbox called a *tiffin-tin*, in large works that draw on the ideas of twenty-first-century conceptual art.

Indian architecture provides a living visual history of the nation's centuries-long past. This is seen throughout India in ancient temples, medieval mosques, colonial architecture, art deco buildings, village huts, and modern skyscrapers.

India has more post offices than any other country.

Dating back to ancient civilizations, Indian architecture has influenced religious structures all over the Eastern world. Features of Indian temples are now prevalent in religious buildings throughout South Asia and East Asia, including the stupa, or temple mound; the pagoda, or temple tower; and the *torana,* or gate.

Each group of people coming to India brought with them new forms of architecture. The Mughals constructed magnificent mosques in the Islamic tradition. One of the buildings, constructed by Mughal emperor Shah Jahan, remains one of the most famous buildings in the world. The Taj Mahal in Agra is an elaborate marble mausoleum constructed as a monument for the king's favorite wife, Mumtaz Mahal. Construction began in 1631. Another historic building is the Rameswaram Temple in Tamil Nadu, which remains an important site for worship of the Hindu gods Shiva and Vishnu. Built in the seventeenth century, the temple is a brilliant example of Dravidian architecture. The Europeans, particularly the Portuguese, built churches similar to the Dravidian temples in their country. Colonial buildings in the English style are also still prevalent throughout India.

India's recent economic boom has supported a wave of new construction that includes skyscrapers, shopping centers, and residences, many with a so-called green or ecologically friendly approach. Some architects have drawn on traditional Indian ideas to build with modern materials. For example, an architect might construct a stepped structure reminiscent of centuries-old south Indian temples in clear, shimmering glass. The Lotus Temple in New Delhi is considered by some the modern Taj Mahal. The dramatic lotus-shaped marble building was built in 1986 as an emblem of peace.

MUSIC AND DANCE

Indian music dates back to the Vedic civilization and includes some of the most complex melodies and instruments in the world. Interrelated with both poetry and religion, Indian music is rooted in the rhythmic chanting of the religious poems in the Vedas.

The two primary forms of classical Indian music are Carnatic from southern India and Hindustani from northern India. The two forms share two elements: the raga, which is a particular pattern of musical notes, and the tala, a rhythm consisting of a number of beats. Both types of music are played by small groups of four to six musicians.

Dancers perform a traditional folk dance.

INDIAN CLOTHING

Traditional Indian clothing is made to withstand the severe heat of the climate. Although clothing can vary by region, traditional wear for women throughout India includes two items: the brightly colored sari, a piece of fabric wrapped as a dress and worn over a blouse and petticoat, and the *salwar kameez*, a long tunic worn with a long scarf over loose-fitting pants. Traditional wear for men includes the dhoti, which are loose-fitting trousers gathered between the legs, and the *lungi*, which drapes like a sarong-style skirt.

Other kinds of religious attire are common in some areas of India, such as the burka, a full-body covering worn by some Muslim women, and the turban, worn by Sikh men. Traditional clothing is still worn throughout India, but more and more frequently, people in urban centers wear a mix of Indian and Western clothing.

Classical Indian music continues to develop today alongside the tradition of folk music. In villages throughout India, folk music is often accompanied by storytelling or other forms of entertainment, such as magic tricks. Indian musicians are also influenced by contemporary music. Pop, rock, and film music, including scores from Indian movies, are all popular in India today.

Indian dance also has classical and folk traditions, which have been enhanced by contemporary developments. Classical Indian dance is divided into types by region and by style. *Manipuri* is a graceful form of dance from Manipur, and *Odissi* is a dramatic dance based on court and temple dances. Classical Indian dance, which has a long and varied tradition, is known for its beautiful and intricate hand gestures and for its dramatic and expressive styles of movement.

LITERATURE AND FILM

Since the first telling of the *Ramayana*, storytelling has been an important part of Indian culture. Performers today entertain village audiences with stories set to music. Their tales are often based on well-loved tales of Hindu deities, much as they have been for centuries. At the same time, storytelling has also taken a more contemporary approach. India produces more movies than any other nation in the world, including the United States.

Fondly nicknamed Bollywood, the Indian film industry makes four times as many movies as Hollywood each year. It also produces movie stars famous in India and the Middle East, such as actress and former Miss World Aishwarya Rai, actor and producer Amitabh Bachchan, and Shah Rukh Khan, who said of Bollywood movies:

THE SHANKAR BROTHERS

Brothers Ravi and Uday Shankar of Bengal brought Indian music and dance to the world. Ravi Shankar (1920–), a world-famous musician and composer, is a master of the sitar, a stringed Indian instrument. His hypnotic ragas have charmed audiences around the globe for more than six decades, including, most famously, the members of the British band the Beatles. Uday Shankar (1900–1977), was a dancer and the founder of a dance troupe. Uday Shankar integrated classical Indian dance with ballet to create a new form. In the 1920s, he danced with the famous Russian ballerina Anna Pavlova.

The world of Hindi films is fantastical, kitsch, and loud. But at the bottom of it all, there are very simple desires—all the hero of a Hindi film really wants is a house for his family, a happy marriage, children who will listen to him. We are not interested in making Armageddon movies.[1]

Indian literature has an equally long and illustrious history of storytelling and is filled with winners of numerous prestigious international prizes. Initially, Indian literature was written in Sanskrit, but it has since been written in nearly every language of India and in English.

The literature of Bengal, in particular, was renowned during the nineteenth century due in large part to the poet, artist, novelist, and philosopher Rabindranath Tagore, the winner of the 1913 Nobel Prize in Literature. Tagore's writing illuminated a universalist worldview that is particular to India—one marked by a love of nature and an understanding of the oneness of all. In addition to writing many novels and poems, Tagore wrote the national anthems of India and of Bangladesh.

Particularly notable among contemporary actors is the internationally famous author Salman Rushdie. He won the Man Booker Prize in 1981 for his expansive novel about India's independence, *Midnight's Children*. In 2008, the Booker went to Indian author Aravind Adiga for his debut novel, *The White Tiger*, an intelligent, empathic, and entertaining story about contemporary India.

Billboards in New Delhi advertise Bollywood films.

CHAPTER 7

POLITICS: A PLURAL DEMOCRACY

Members of the largest democracy in the world are deeply engaged in local and international issues. In fact, according to the well-traveled writers of *Lonely Planet: India*, the most popular topic of conversation in India is politics, beating out cricket matches and Bollywood stars for inspiring the most animated local talk.

Perhaps it should not come as a surprise that Indians scrutinize the beliefs and activities of their leaders and the world. Although India's history is long, the nation in its modern form is relatively young. The Constitution of India was adopted on January 26, 1950, shortly after the country's independence from the United Kingdom, and it has been amended often since. Indians share a historic culture and a new democracy and are in the midst of a period of tremendous growth.

Muslim men joined a protest over India's rule in Kashmir in September 2010.

Even though the democracy is young, the political struggles that India faces today are not new. For the most part, differing opinions and religions have cohabited peaceably. But at times, regional and religious factions have threatened India's unity.

Hindus have been in India since the second century BCE and Muslims since before Babur, the first Mughal leader, took over in the sixteenth century. Although they have lived together harmoniously much of the time, each working in governments and armies run by the other, tensions have developed between members of the two religions.

These tensions came to a head at the dawn of the secular nation's independence. In 1945, two years before the end

JAWAHARLAL NEHRU

Jawaharlal Nehru was a charismatic leader during India's struggle for independence and the first prime minister of the Republic of India. Nehru was born in Allahabad on November 14, 1889. His father was an attorney, and his mother worked at home to raise Nehru and his two sisters. Nehru attended schools in India and England, training to become an attorney like his father. Upon returning to India, Nehru was attracted to the teachings of Mohandas Gandhi. With Gandhi's encouragement, he practiced yoga and studied the Vedas. Nehru rose to prominence on the political scene and was elected leader of the Indian National Congress in the 1920s. Nehru served as president of Congress and India's first prime minister until his death on May 27, 1964.

The flag of India is orange, white, and green with a circular blue design in the center.

of the British Raj, India's two main political parties disagreed about how to proceed as a unified nation. The Congress Party, led by Jawaharlal Nehru, wanted to form a united India, while the Muslim League, led by Mohammed Ali Jinnah, wanted to form a separate Islamic state. One of the British viceroy's last acts was to attempt to settle the dispute by dividing India.

The British enacted the partition of India in 1947, splitting off a part of northern India around East Bengal and Punjab to create the nation of Pakistan. The result was violence and bloodshed on both sides, with Hindus fleeing the newly Islamic nation and Muslims leaving India to get to Pakistan.

One of the first acts of the newly independent India was to go to war with Pakistan from 1947 to 1948. The war failed to settle the

PRATIBHA DEVISINGH PATIL

Pratibha Devisingh Patil was the first woman to be elected president of India. She was born on December 19, 1934, in the village of Nadgaon in Maharashtra. After becoming a lawyer, she began her career at Jalgaon District Court, where she also devoted time to social services with an emphasis on helping poor women. At 27, she was elected to the Maharashtra State Legislature. She was reelected four times before serving as a member of both houses of parliament and, immediately prior to assuming the presidency, as governor of Rajasthan.

The Indian Parliament building in New Delhi

dispute over the state of Kashmir, which had been taken over by India but claimed by Pakistan. A second war between the two countries in 1965 ended with cease-fire mandated by the United Nations. India went to war with Pakistan again in 1971, which resulted in the formation of Bangladesh from East Pakistan, and the countries barely avoided another fight in 2002.

THE STRUCTURE OF THE WORLD'S MOST POPULOUS DEMOCRACY

India is a democratic federal republic, a union of states governed by a constitution. The nation's president is the chief of state, and its prime minister is the head of government. This means the president represents the country in official ceremonies and in dealings with other nations, while the prime minister makes decisions for the government.

STRUCTURE OF THE GOVERNMENT OF INDIA

Executive Branch		Legislative Branch	Judicial Branch
President and Vice President	Prime Minister and Cabinet	Rajya Sabha (Council of States) Lok Sabha (House of the People)	Supreme Court lower courts

India's first female president was Pratibha Devisingh Patil.

INDIRA GANDHI

Among India's most famous leaders was Prime Minister Indira Gandhi, one of the first women in the world to be elected leader of a large democracy. The daughter of India's first prime minister, Jawaharlal Nehru, Indira became involved in politics from a young age. She was a prominent member of a children's group called the Monkey Brigade, which helped warn Indians of pending arrests during the fight for independence from Great Britain, and she joined the Indian National Congress in 1938.

In 1942, Indira married Indian journalist Feroze Gandhi, with whom she had two sons. When her father became prime minister in 1947, she aided him in hosting political events in place of her mother, who had died in 1936.

Gandhi remained active in Indian politics, and in 1966, after the death of India's second prime minister, Lal Bahadur Shastri, she was appointed to replace him. She became prime minister again in 1967 and in 1971 when the Indian public voted her party into power. Her party lost the election of 1977, but returned to power in 1980, granting Gandhi her final term as prime minister. She remained in office until she was killed by a Sikh bodyguard on October 31, 1984. The assassination occurred shortly after a clash between Sikh militants and the Indian army inside a Sikh temple.

The president and vice president are elected by the members of the state legislatures and both houses of Parliament. In 2011, India's president was Pratibha Devisingh Patil. Upon taking office on July 25, 2007, she become India's twelfth president and the first woman elected to this office. The president then appoints the members of the cabinet.

In 2011, India's prime minister was Manmohan Singh. He took office on May 22, 2004. The prime minister is selected by the majority party of Parliament.

Parliament consists of the *Rajya Sabha*, or the Council of States, and the *Lok Sabha*, or the House of the People. The Council of States is limited by the Indian constitution to 250 members: 12 appointed by the president and the rest chosen by elected members of state governments to represent all the states and the two territories. The House of the People has 545 seats. Almost all are elected by the people to represent the states and the union territories. Two are appointed by the president, at his or her discretion, from the Anglo-Indian community. The president may make this decision to achieve greater diversity, should he or she feel that this group has not been adequately represented in the House.

Each of the 28 states has a chief minister, a governor, and a legislature. Each state government is structured similarly to the federal government, with a legislative parliament and a Council of Ministers led by a chief minister. The chief minister, elected by the people, essentially runs the state. The Indian president appoints the state's governor.

India has lived under Hindu law for thousands of years. Upon gaining independence from the United Kingdom, India established a judicial branch with a supreme court and a system of lower courts. The judicial branch is separate from the executive and legislative branches of the government. The Supreme Court consists of one chief justice and 25 associate justices who are all appointed by the president.

The Indian Constitution is the longest written constitution in the world.

India's many political parties give voice to a variety of opinions and perspectives. However, the existence of so many parties can also make

Indians rally to support Sonia Gandhi, whose image appears on her supporters' flag.

for cumbersome elections, given the large number of names on the ballot. The nation's oldest political party is the Indian National Congress, which in 2011 was led by Sonia Gandhi (no relation to Mohandas Gandhi). Other political parties include the Bharatiya Janata Party (BJP), a Hindu nationalist party; the Communist Party of India; and Janata Dal, a secular and liberal or left-wing party.

Democracies the world over allow for equitable and participatory governance. But Indians, in particular, have embraced elections as opportunities for equality, electing a woman as the current president, twice electing Indira Gandhi as prime minister, and electing people from lower castes to offices of government.

A large democracy can have drawbacks, including the unwieldy size of governmental bureaucracy. India's pluralistic democracy presents both benefits and challenges, offering diversity and voicing many perspectives. But with so many small political parties, it can be difficult to reach consensus.

To this day, India remains in a bitter political dispute with Pakistan over the state of Kashmir.

KOCHERIL RAMAN NARAYANAN

Indians were proud to have elected Kocheril Raman Narayanan, a Dalit, to the office of president on July 25, 1997. They felt a sense of national success in electing to the highest office a man of the lowest caste. Narayanan is still commonly referred to as India's first "untouchable president," signaling the deep significance of his election and the decisive blow it dealt to the centuries-old social structure.[1]

ATTACKS ON MUMBAI

On November 26, 2008, gunmen attacked several sites in Mumbai, killing at least 160 people and injuring more than 300.[3] Setting off a reign of terror that lasted three days, the gunmen began at the popular Leopold Café and proceeded to attack targets that included a train station, a hospital, and two luxury hotels: the historic Taj Mahal Palace and the Oberoi Trident, where people were taken hostage. The gunmen are believed to have arrived in Mumbai by water, hijacking a fishing boat and entering through the crowded harbor. The well-planned attack was carried out with automatic weapons and grenades. Indian police and antiterrorism units responded immediately but were strained to the limits of their abilities.

The Indian government blamed the attacks on Pakistan, further straining relations between the two countries. The Pakistani government stated that it had no knowledge of the attacks.

Both nations have had nuclear weapons capabilities since the 1980s, raising the stakes of the conflict. In addition to the struggle with Pakistan, India has faced increased struggles within its own borders, as groups such as the Shiv Sena political party and some Islamic groups have sought greater power. Religious extremists have assassinated several Indian leaders, including Mohandas Gandhi in 1948; Indira Gandhi, the country's first female prime minister, in 1984; and Rajiv Gandhi, former prime minister and Indira's son, in 1991. Extremists have also attacked Indian targets on many occasions, including planting a series of bombs on trains in 2006 that killed almost 200 people.[2]

Indira Gandhi arriving at Parliament in New Delhi, 1978

CHAPTER 8

ECONOMICS: A NEW SUPERPOWER?

India has experienced a fantastic economic boom over the past two decades. Since 1997, its economy has grown an average of 7 percent a year, making it one of the world's fastest-growing economies and putting India on track to becoming an economic superpower.[1]

But economic growth has not come evenly to all of India. Historically, India has one of the highest poverty rates in the world. Even today, with the nation's current economic boom, an estimated 220 million Indians live below the poverty line.[2] Half of Indian children under the age of five are undernourished.[3] How is it that so many people still live in poverty in a nation with such tremendous economic success? A variety of factors explain this situation.

A man farms using traditional methods.

TECH BOOM

Since the 1990s, India has developed a thriving information technology (IT) industry, including renowned software companies and international call centers. The boom has changed the landscape and economic prospects of many Indian cities.

Indian software companies have grown to rival the world's best producers of software. Indian scientists and engineers have long worked in the United States, and many have returned home to fuel the growth of their nation's industry. So many computer companies have sprung up in the city of Hyderabad in the state of Andhra Pradesh that it has been nicknamed "Cyberabad." Bangalore and other cities in the state of Karnataka have also become significant players in the technology and software industry.

International call centers have also brought jobs to many English-speaking Indians and are considered part of the IT sector. Employees go through training to learn basic phrases and cultural cues from American or Australian English. Working in call centers set up in India, these individuals respond to service calls from people in Western nations—primarily in the United States and Australia. The international companies pay Indians less than they would people in their home countries in a process called outsourcing.

One factor is that people in different areas of India lead very different lives. People in the cities tend to be more educated and have access to new job opportunities, but people in the rural villages tend to live much as they have for centuries. Much of the recent economic development has come from taking advantage of opportunities in technology and industry—sectors of the economy that have not reached Indian villages for the most part.

India's economic growth has been due primarily to government decisions made throughout the 1990s to loosen restriction on trade and business. As a result, Indian businesses expanded and

Many members of India's growing middle class work
in the technology industry.

A woman begs on the streets of Jaipur.

those in other nations, particularly the United States and Australia, began to hire Indian labor at a lower cost.

The jobs that opened up as a result have provided opportunities mostly for people who are educated. Those who speak English can work in large call centers established by US companies in New Delhi and other cities. India's many talented engineers and scientists can find employment in the growing technology centers in Hyderabad and Bangalore. But only one-fifth of Indians work at jobs in the growing industrial, technology, and commercial sectors.[4]

Thus, India's economic boom has created a large middle class but left others out of the growth.

India's labor force is 478 million strong—the second largest in the world—and 52 percent of Indians work in agriculture.[5] Many of these workers still tend small farms in villages, leading lives not so different from their ancestors. But others have shifted to commercial farming, an industry that has grown significantly since the 1970s, when the government introduced chemical fertilizers and pesticides. India's agricultural products include rice, wheat, oilseed, cotton, jute, tea, sugarcane, lentils, onions, potatoes, dairy products, sheep, goats, poultry, and fish.

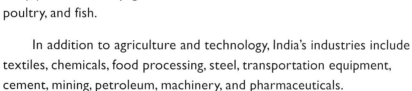

EMPLOYMENT IN INDIA

The majority of Indians work in agriculture, which makes up 17.1 percent of the nation's gross national product (GDP). Thirty-four percent work in the services industry, which makes up a little more than one-half of the GDP, 54.6 percent. Only 14 percent of Indians are employed in the industrial sector, which makes up 28.2 percent of the GDP.[6]

In addition to agriculture and technology, India's industries include textiles, chemicals, food processing, steel, transportation equipment, cement, mining, petroleum, machinery, and pharmaceuticals.

Resources of India

Legend:
- Cereal Crops
- Fishing
- Iron and Steel
- Livestock
- Manufacturing
- Rice
- Tea
- Textiles

ENVIRONMENT AND RESOURCES

India's rich natural environment draws visitors from around the world, but its growing industries and large population have taken a huge toll on the nation's natural resources. Timber, for example, has been depleted significantly through deforestation to make space for urbanization, factories, and industry. Additional natural resources include coal, petroleum products, precious stones, and iron and steel.

As India's own resources are depleted, it imports a significant amount of fuel in the form of crude oil to keep its large cities and busy industries going. India is the fifth-largest consumer of oil in the world.[7] Other significant imports include machinery, fertilizer, and chemicals for the agriculture industry. Three of India's own natural resources—iron, steel, and precious stones—are also its primary imports.

India has 670 million cell phones, the second most in the world.

One of India's exports in recent decades has been computer software, for which the nation is gaining an international reputation. Other exports include petroleum products, precious stones, machinery, chemicals, vehicles, apparel, and iron and steel. India's main trading partners are the United Arab Emirates, China, and the United States.

HYDROELECTRICITY

India is the sixth-largest producer and consumer of electricity in the world.[9] In an effort to produce more renewable electricity, the government has started a number of hydroelectric projects, damming rivers to generate electricity. In addition to making electricity, these large construction projects irrigate thousands of villages, many of them near desert areas. These projects are also controversial, however, because dam construction has flooded some villages and displaced large numbers of people. Dams can also cause damage to river ecosystems.

CHALLENGES AHEAD

As India surges ahead in the twenty-first century, international economists routinely refer to it as an emergent superpower. However, the nation will continue to face the challenges of maintaining its deteriorating natural environment and finding ways to bring its large and growing population into the economic growth. With 10.8 percent unemployment and a per capita GDP of $3,400 in 2010, India faces a widening divide between the rich and the poor.[8] In addition to a high rate of poverty, social challenges include providing access to education for its large population. The depletion of natural resources is also quickly becoming a social problem, as India seeks ways to provide clean drinking water to its whole population.

Some Indian residents have poor access to clean water.

Similar to other industrialized nations, India must find ways to balance environmental protection with a fast-growing industry sector and a ballooning economy. India's large population adds another level to this issue of balance, straining the nation's natural resources, food production, and employment. On the other hand, the large size of the population—combined with the people's dedication to education, work, family, and spirituality—have also fueled the economic growth and provided a large pool of talent and ingenuity to come up with creative solutions to these challenges.

INDIAN MONEY

The State Bank of India Group is the largest bank in India and one of the largest in the world. Indian currency is the rupee. One US dollar equals between 45 and 47 Indian rupees.

India's currency is the rupee.

CHAPTER 9
INDIA TODAY

India has embraced the future with open arms. Its fast-growing economy is fueled by industrious businesses and cutting-edge software, and the government has made significant efforts to equalize opportunities and abandon the caste system. But at the same time, India's centuries-old past lives on in day-to-day life and traditions. Family and religion remain the cornerstones of Indian life.

The Hindu religion sees life as divided into four stages—childhood, student life, family life, and old age—and each has its own set of goals and responsibilities. These stages have defined the way of life for India's large Hindu population for centuries. Even today, the family is the main unit of society. Beyond that, caste still plays a role in many rural areas, with a person's caste status defining many aspects of his or her life. In rural areas and beyond, community also plays a role in defining a person's public roles and private relationships. Indians tend to remain connected to their home villages even after moving away.

An Indian couple celebrates their engagement in a traditional ceremony.

LOVE MARRIAGES

Traditional Indian marriages are arranged, but more and more people in the cities are stepping away from that age-old custom to enter into what are called love marriages. In these unions, the bride and groom choose one another. They marry for love, rather than as a family or economic arrangement. The most radical couples even disregard caste, marrying the person they love without regard to his or her background.

Throughout India, families follow a patriarchal structure, in which a male is the head of the family and heritage is traced through the father's ancestry. In Hindu culture, wives are traditionally expected to be devoted to their husbands, and male children are generally valued over female children. This patriarchal structure is supported by marriage customs. Marriages are customarily arranged by families rather than decided by a couple independently.

The wife's family is then expected to give a large dowry, or financial gift, to the husband's family, which makes daughters a heavy financial burden to their families. Dating, romance, and public displays of affection are frowned on in India.

For Muslim Indian families, arranged marriages are also the custom. But in these marriages, the husband is expected to promise to care for the wife and provide her with wealth, so the woman's dowry is balanced by the man's responsibility.

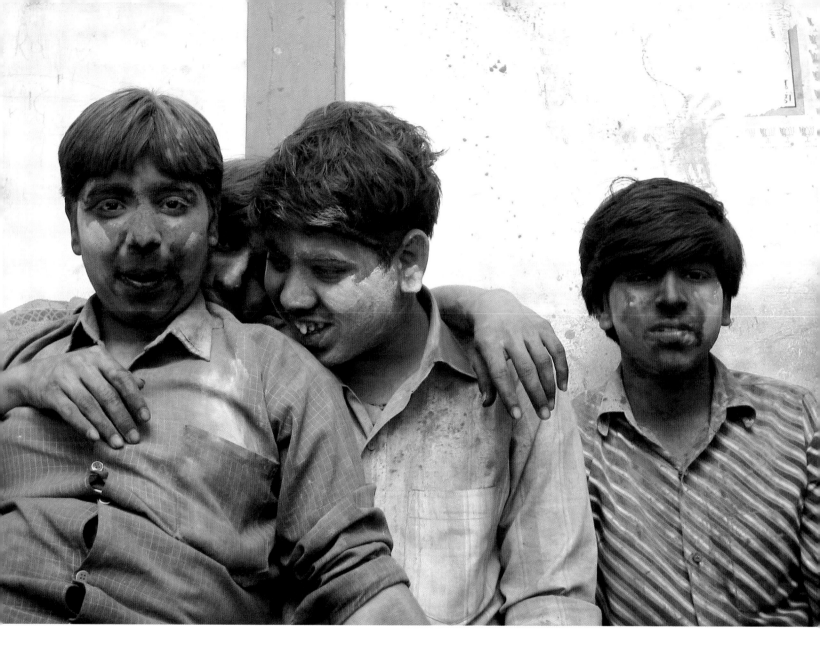

Boys celebrate the Holi Festival in Jaipur by throwing colored powders at each other.

Work ethic and education are important to the Indian culture, as are celebrations and making time for religion, leisure, family life, and art. In these areas, too, the new and the old blend, as traditional Indian arts are enjoyed along with contemporary films and music. However, even as contemporary culture and technology have infiltrated India, the national lifestyle, cuisine, and clothing styles have remained dominant.

TEENAGERS IN INDIA

Indian teenagers are influenced by the traditional emphasis on family and religion. Teens are expected to do well in school, to spend time with family, and to remain chaste. But similar to teens everywhere, Indian teens find ways to challenge the boundaries of their cultures. Even though dating is generally disallowed, teens in many cities have begun to use texting as a way to experiment with romantic relationships.

In India, it is impolite to eat with the left hand.

Indian teens enjoy movies, music, and the Internet, but their contemporary culture tends to be made in India and so reflects Indian values. Movies and television programs do not show nudity, and even kissing scenes are rare.

Indian families have traditionally lived in large, extended clans, with the wife moving in with her husband's family after marriage. Most teenagers in rural

Children wearing a mix of traditional and Western clothes walk to school.

TEEN SUICIDE

Since the early part of the twenty-first century, disturbing reports have shown an increase in teen suicide in India. A 2004 report from the journal *New Scientist* showed that teens in southern India had the highest rate of suicide in the world. According to the report, "The average suicide rate for young women aged between 15 to 19 living around Vellore in Tamil Nadu was 148 per 100,000. This compares to just 2.1 suicides per 100,000 in the same group in the [United Kingdom]."[1]

More recently, in 2010, the BBC News reported that suicide among Indian teens had become more prevalent across India. For example, suicide has increased dramatically in the developed state of Maharashtra and its cosmopolitan capital, Mumbai. The first 26 days of January witnessed 32 teen suicides in the region—more than one a day.[2]

Girls make up the majority of suicide victims, but both boys and girls are affected. Concerned authorities cite the constant pressure to succeed and the changing family structure as potential reasons for teens' suicide. Resources for troubled youths include a helpline called Aasra and an information campaign, Life is Beautiful, aimed at helping teens recognize that there is more to life than school and achievement.

areas still live in large family units like this, but urban teens increasingly live with only their parents and siblings. They likely visit their extended families during celebrations.

Just as the nation as a whole has done, Indian teens embrace both new and old, wearing both traditional and Western-style clothing. In the cities, Western-style clothing is common, but teens still wear traditional dress for festivals. In villages in rural India, traditional Indian clothing is the norm for teens as well as adults.

EDUCATION IN INDIA

Education is highly valued in Indian culture, but it is not equally accessible to all. In particular, girls attend less school on average than boys. Most Indian children attend primary school, but after that, attendance declines. Only about one-half of all Indian students ages 11 through 14 attend school.[3]

SCHOOL IN INDIA

The majority of Indian children attend primary school, but many of them do not go on to secondary school. Nearly 54 percent of all Indian children attend preprimary school, and slightly more than 91 percent attend primary school. Almost 95 percent of students who attend primary school graduate.[5]

The Constitution of India decrees that all children under age 14 receive a free education, and the average length of time spent in school is ten years. Yet while 73.4 percent of all Indian boys are literate, or able to read and write by the age of 15, only 47.8 percent of girls are literate.[4] Literacy is also higher in urban areas than rural areas.

Initially, the Indian government gave the responsibility for education to the states, but due to a constitutional amendment, both levels of government now share the responsibility. The federal government has made significant efforts to ensure that girls receive an equal education to boys—for instance, funding programs to educate girls and promoting initiatives to encourage girls to attend and to stay in school.

Both the federal and state governments run India's universities and colleges. Although the majority of students do not attend college, those who do have many options. During the first 40 years after the nation achieved independence, the government put a strong focus on building universities and institutions of higher learning.

LOOKING TO THE FUTURE

India is still a developing nation, and it is growing rapidly and successfully. But the challenges it faces now will only increase with its growing population. India is challenged to provide adequate health care, education, and employment opportunities for all its citizens. Specifically, the HIV/AIDS epidemic has hit India hard in the twenty-first century. Providing clean drinking water for everyone is another challenge, given the country's large population and encroaching urbanization.

AIDS EPIDEMIC IN INDIA

Avert, an international HIV/AIDS charity, states that the first case of HIV was reported in India in 1986. Since then, HIV and AIDS have spread throughout India. Today, approximately 2.3 million people in India are HIV positive. Of these individuals, 39 percent are female and 3.5 percent are children.[6]

India is striving to decrease poverty and improve living conditions for its growing population.

Caring for the environment while continuing to develop industry will be another significant challenge for India as it moves into a new era. The serious environmental costs of India's rapid industrial development and growing population are straining its natural bounty and diversity. Widespread poverty and an ongoing and difficult political struggle with Pakistan over Kashmir are primary challenges.

India has the fifth-highest GDP in the world.

Despite all this, the outlook for India's future is very bright. The nation is experiencing rapid growth, and it is predicted with China to be one of the world's next great superpowers. If India can harness the energy and vibrancy of its diverse population, it could prove a powerful example for all the world of the power of pluralism.

Indians can call on their legendary history and diverse people to build themselves a prosperous future.

TIMELINE

Ca. 3,000 BCE	The Indus valley civilization constructs the first urban centers in the region.
1500–500 BCE	The Vedic civilization in the Indo-Gangetic Plain speaks an early version of Sanskrit and develops the Hindu sacred texts.
321–185 BCE	The Maurya Empire establishes the first Indian empire, in which the whole country is united under one government.
500 BCE	Buddhism and Jainism are founded in India.
320–510 CE	The Gupta Empire nourishes the arts and literature during the Golden Age of India.
1498	Vasco da Gama, a Portuguese sailor, arrives in India.
1510	The Portuguese take control of Goa.
1526	Babur establishes the first Mughal Empire of India with Islamic rule in the region.
1600	Queen Elizabeth allows the British East India Company to trade with India.
1631	The Mughal emperor Shah Jahan begins construction on the Taj Mahal, an elaborate mausoleum and memorial for his deceased wife Mumtaz Mahal.
1707	Aurangzeb, the last great Mughal ruler, dies.
1857	The Indian Mutiny or the First War of Independence begins in Uttar Pradesh on May 10.

1858	British colonizers take power over the government of India.
1869	Mohandas Gandhi is born on October 2.
1885	The Indian National Congress is formed.
1919	On April 13, British forces attack and kill unarmed Indian protesters in Amritsar.
1947	On August 15, India achieves independence from the United Kingdom and resumes self-government.
1948	On January 30, Mohandas Gandhi is assassinated in New Delhi.
1950	On January 26, the Constitution of India is ratified.
1966	Indira Gandhi begins the first of her four terms as prime minister.
1984	On October 31, Prime Minister Indira Gandhi is assassinated by one of her Sikh bodyguards.
2007	On July 25, India's first woman president, Pratibha Patil, takes office.
2006	On November 26, a series of terrorist bombings occurs in Mumbai, killing nearly 200 people.
2011	India wins the Cricket World Cup.

FACTS AT YOUR FINGERTIPS

GEOGRAPHY

Official name: Republic of India
(in Hindi, Bharatiya Ganarajya)

Area: 1,269,219 square miles
(3,287,263 sq km)

Climate: Varied; cold in the
northern Himalayan Mountains, hot
and dry in the deserts of Rajasthan
and Gujarat, and hot and wet in
southern India.

Highest elevation: Kanchenjunga,
third-highest peak in the world,
28,209 feet (8,598 m) above sea
level

Lowest elevation: Indian Ocean, 0
feet (0 m) above sea level

Significant geographic features:
Himalayan Mountains, Ganges River,
Thar Desert

PEOPLE

Population (July 2011 est.):
1,189,172,906, the second-largest in
the world

Most populous city: Mumbai

Ethnic groups: Indo-Aryan, 72
percent; Dravidian or native, 25
percent; Mongoloid (with ancestors
from northern Asia), 3 percent

Percentage of residents living in
urban areas: 30 percent

Life expectancy: 66.8 years at birth
(world rank: 162)

Languages: Hindi and English; the
Indian government recognizes 14
additional official languages. Each
of the 28 states also has an official
language.

Religion(s): Hindu, 80.5 percent;
Muslim, 13.4 percent; Christian, 2.3
percent; Sikh, 1.9 percent; other, 1.8
percent; unspecified, 0.1 percent

GOVERNMENT AND ECONOMY

Government: federal republic

Capital: New Delhi

Date of adoption of current constitution: January 26, 1950

Head of state: president

Head of government: prime minister

Legislature: The *Rajya Sabha*, or the Council of States (no more than 250 members), and the *Lok Sabha,* or the House of the People (545 members).

Currency: rupee

Industries and natural resources: agriculture, technology (software), petroleum, tourism, information technology, and iron and steel.

NATIONAL SYMBOLS

Holidays: Republic Day, January 26, commemorates India's constitution, which was ratified on this day in 1950.

Flag: Consists of three horizontal stripes of equal size: the top one is orange, the middle one white, and the bottom one green. In the center of the white stripe is a navy blue wheel, or chakra in Sanskrit, with 24 spokes.

National anthem: "Jana Gana Mana," or "Thou Art the Ruler of the Minds of All People," written by Nobel Prize laureate Rabindranath Tagore and adopted in 1950.

National animal: Bengal tiger

National bird: Peacock

KEY PEOPLE

Mohandas Gandhi (1869–1948), also known as Mahatma Gandhi or Great Soul, was a lawyer, an activist, and a spiritual and political leader of India's independence from Great Britain.

Rabindranath Tagore (1861–1941) was an Indian novelist, poet, activist, and philosopher.

FACTS AT YOUR FINGERTIPS CONTINUED

Jawaharlal Nehru (1889–1964) served as the first prime minister of the Republic of India.

Indira Gandhi (1917–1984), daughter of Jawaharlal Nehru, was prime minister of India from 1966 to 1977 and 1980 to 1984.

STATES AND TERRITORIES OF INDIA

State; Capital

Andhra Pradesh; Hyderabad

Arunachal Pradesh; Itanagar

Assam (Asom); Dispur

Bihar; Patna

Chhattisgarh; Raipur

Delhi (National Capital Territory); Delhi

Goa; Panaji

Gujarat; Gandhinagar

Haryana; Chandigarh

Himachal Pradesh; Shimla

Jammu and Kashmir; Jammu (winter), Srinagar (summer)

Jharkhand; Ranchi

Karnataka; Bangalore

Kerala; Thiruvananthapuram

Madhya Pradesh; Bhopal

Maharashtra; Mumbai

Manipur; Imphal

Meghalaya; Shillong

Mizoram; Aizawl

Nagaland; Kohima

Orissa (Odisha); Bhubaneshwar

Punjab; Chandigarh

Rajasthan; Jaipur

Sikkim; Gangtok

Tamil Nadu; Chennai

Tripura; Agartala

Uttar Pradesh; Lucknow

Uttarakhand; Dehra Dun

West Bengal; Kolkata

Union Territory; Capital

Andaman and Nicobar; Port Blair

Chandigarh; Chandigarh

Dadra and Nagar Haveli; Silvassa

Daman and Diu; Daman

Lakshadweep; Kavaratti

Puducherry; Puducherry

GLOSSARY

ahimsa

A Sanskrit word for the ancient Hindu principle of nonviolence or nonharm.

Anglicized

Adapted to English language or culture.

Aryan

A Sanskrit word that designates the Indo-European ethnic group; means "noble."

call center

A business where service calls are answered.

colonization

The process of taking over rule of a region or nation through political or military means.

deciduous

A type of plant or tree that sheds its leaves annually.

gross domestic product

A measure of a country's economy; the total of all goods and services produced in a country in a year.

indigenous

Coming originally or naturally from an area.

monsoon

The wind stream over the Indian ocean blowing southwest in summer and northwest in winter; also the season of heavy rainstorms that crosses India from June through December.

Mughal

A leader descended from a conquering Islamic tribe; also *Mogul*.

Sanskrit

An ancient Indo-European language and the spiritual language of Hinduism.

sari

A draped cloth garment.

secular

Nonreligious.

subcontinent

A landmass that is a subdivision of a continent.

tectonic plates

The huge pieces that make up Earth's crust; the way plates shift causes earthquakes and geologic instability.

ADDITIONAL RESOURCES

SELECTED BIBLIOGRAPHY

Singh, Sarina. *Lonely Planet: India.* Victoria, Austral.: Lonely Planet, 2009. Print.

Tharoor, Shashi. *The Elephant, the Tiger, and the Cell Phone: Reflections on India, the Emerging 21st Century Superpower.* New York: Arcade, 2007. Print.

FURTHER READINGS

Rushdie, Salman. *Midnight's Children.* New York: Random, 2006. Print.

Schomp, Virginia. *Ancient India.* New York: Scholastic, 2005. Print.

Vander Hook, Sue. *Mahatma Gandhi: Proponent of Peace.* Edina, MN: ABDO, 2010. Print.

WEB LINKS

To learn more about India, visit ABDO Publishing Company online at **www.abdopublishing.com**. Web sites about India are featured on our Book Links page. These links are routinely monitored and updated to provide the most current information available.

PLACES TO VISIT

If you are ever in India, consider checking out these important and interesting sites!

Rameswaram Temple

Rameswaram Temple, on the island of Rameswaram in Tamil Nadu, is one example of many Hindu temples in southern India. The island is home to temples and palaces built from the twelfth to the sixteenth centuries.

Sanjay Gandhi State Park

The Sanjay Gandhi State Park lies about one and one-half hours north of the city of Mumbai in Maharashtra State. It is one of India's 97 national parks.

Taj Mahal

The Taj Mahal is located in Agra, India, which is south of New Delhi in the state of Uttar Pradesh. The landmark mausoleum, palace, and garden were constructed by the Mughal ruler Shah Jahan in memory of his deceased and beloved wife.

SOURCE NOTES

CHAPTER 1. A VISIT TO INDIA

1. "Karachi Is Asia's Largest Slum, not Dharavi: UNDP." *The Times of India.* Bennett, Coleman & Co., 6 Sept. 2009. Web. 8 Feb. 2011.

2. "Life in a Slum." BBC News. BBC, 2011. Web. 8 Feb. 2011.

3. Shashi Tharoor. *The Elephant, the Tiger, and the Cell Phone: Reflections on India, the Emerging 21rst Century Superpower.* New York: Arcade, 2007. Print. 8.

CHAPTER 2. GEOGRAPHY: A LAND OF VARIETY

1. "The World Factbook: India." *Central Intelligence Agency.* Central Intelligence Agency, 12 Jan. 2011. Web. 19 Jan. 2011.

2. "Country Guide: India." *BBC: Weather.* BBC, n.d. Web. 19 Jan. 2011.

3. "India." *Encyclopædia Britannica.* Encyclopædia Britannica, 2011. Web. 19 Jan. 2011.

4. Ratnajyoti Dutta. "Monsoon Winds Up on Positive Note, Crops Gain." *Reuters.* Reuters, 30 Sept. 2010. Web. 19 Jan. 2011.

5. "Roof of the World and the Abode of Snow." *Visible Earth.* NASA, 25 Feb. 2008. Web. 19 Jan. 2011.

6. "Himalayas." *Encyclopædia Britannica.* Encyclopedia Britannica, 2011. Web. 19 Jan. 2011.

7. "Roof of the World and the Abode of Snow." *Visible Earth.* NASA, 25 Feb. 2008. Web. 19 Jan. 2011.

CHAPTER 3. ANIMALS AND NATURE: RICH BIODIVERSITY

1. Sarina Singh. *Lonely Planet: India.* Victoria, Austral.: Lonely Planet, 2009. Print. 99.

2. "Panthera tigris ssp. tigris." *The IUCN Red List of Threatened Species.* International Union for Conservation of Nature and Natural Resources, 2010. Web. 19 Jan. 2011.

3. Satish Jacob. "A Holy Call to Spare the Tiger." ABC News International. ABC News.com, 7 Mar. 2006. Web. 19 Jan. 2011.

4. Sarina Singh. *Lonely Planet: India.* Victoria, Austral.: Lonely Planet, 2009. Print. 96.

5. Ibid.

6. "India." *Encyclopedia Britannica.* Encyclopædia Britannica, 2011. Web. 19 Jan. 2011.

7. "Summary Statistics: Summaries by Country, Table 5, Threatened Species in Each Country." *IUCN Red List of Threatened Species.* International Union for Conservation of Nature and Natural Resources, 2010. Web. 18 Jan. 2011.

8. Sarina Singh. *Lonely Planet: India.* Victoria, Austral.: Lonely Planet, 2009. Print. 102.

9. Ibid

10. "Wildlife." *India.gov.in.* National Informatics Centre, Government of India, 7 Dec. 2010. Web. 9 Feb. 2011.

11. "Biosphere Reserves." *Wildlife Institute of India.* Wildlife Institute of India, n.d. Web. 9 Feb. 2010.

CHAPTER 4. HISTORY: AN EPIC PAST

1. Sarina Singh. Lonely Planet: India. Victoria, Austral.: Lonely Planet, 2009. Print. 272.

2. P. N. Chopra. *A Comprehensive History of Modern India.* New Delhi, India: Sterling, 2005. Google Book Search. Web. 19 Jan. 2011.

SOURCE NOTES CONTINUED

CHAPTER 5. PEOPLE: DIVERSE YET UNITED

1. Shashi Tharoor. *India: From Midnight to the Millennium and Beyond.* New York: Arcade, 1997. Print. 13.

2. "The World Factbook: India." *Central Intelligence Agency.* Central Intelligence Agency, 8 Mar. 2011. Web. 14 Mar. 2011.

3. Ibid.

4. Ibid.

5. Ibid.

6. Ibid.

7. Ibid.

CHAPTER 6. CULTURE: A COLORFUL NATION

1. Ammu Kannampilly. "Bollywood Rising: India's Biggest Movie Star Shah Rukh Khan." *ABC News International.* ABC News.com, 23 June 2007. Web. 19 Jan. 2011.

CHAPTER 7. POLITICS: A PLURAL DEMOCRACY

1. P. J. Anthony. "K. R. Narayanan Dies at 85; 'Untouchable' India President." *New York Times.* New York Times, 10 Nov. 2005. Web. 19 Jan. 2011.

2. Saritha Rai and Somini Sengupta. "Train Bombs in India Kill Scores." *New York Times.* New York Times, 11 July 2006. Web. 9 Feb. 2011.

3. "What Is Known about the Mumbai Attacks." *CNN News.* Cable News Network, 28 Nov. 2008. Web. 19 Jan. 2011.

CHAPTER 8. ECONOMICS: A NEW SUPERPOWER?

1. "The World Factbook: India." *Central Intelligence Agency*. Central Intelligence Agency, 12 Jan. 2011. Web. 19 Jan. 2011.

2. Sarina Singh. *Lonely Planet: India*. Victoria, Austral.: Lonely Planet, 2009. Print. 65.

3. Vikas Bajaj. "Galloping Growth, and Hunger in India." *New York Times*. New York Times, 11 Feb. 2011. Web. 11 Feb. 2011.

4. "India." Encyclopedia Britannica. Encyclopedia Britannica, 2011. Web. 19 Jan. 2011.

5. "The World Factbook: India." *Central Intelligence Agency*. Central Intelligence Agency, 12 Jan. 2011. Web. 19 Jan. 2011.

6. Ibid.

7. Ibid.

8. Ibid.

9. Ibid.

CHAPTER 9. INDIA TODAY

1. Shaoni Bhattacharya. "Indian Teens Have World's Highest Suicide Rate. *New Scientist*. Reed Business Information, 2 Apr. 2004. Web. 19 Jan. 2011.

2. Zubair Ahmed. "Alarm at Mumbai's Teenage Suicide Trend." *BBC News*. BBC, 1 Feb. 2010. Web. 19 Jan. 2011.

3. "India." *Encyclopedia Britannica*. Encyclopædia Britannica, 2011. Web. 19 Jan. 2011.

4. "The World Factbook: India." *Central Intelligence Agency*. Central Intelligence Agency, 12 Jan. 2011. Web. 19 Jan. 2011.

5. "Education Statistics Version 5.3." *EdStats*. World Bank, 2011. Web. 19 Jan. 2011.

6. "India HIV & AIDS Statistics." *Avert*. Avert, 2011. Web. 19 Jan. 2011.

INDEX

INDEX CONTINUED

PHOTO CREDITS

Andrew Lee/Fotolia, cover, 128 (bottom); Pawel Pietraszewski/Shutterstock Images, 2, 10; iStockphoto, 5 (top), 5 (bottom), 15, 33, 39, 63, 72, 95, 124, 127, 130; Falk Kienas/Shutterstock Images, 5 (middle), 18, 64, 127, 133; Nickolay Stanev/Shutterstock Images, 6; Matt Kania/Map Hero, Inc., 9, 21, 23, 60, 110; Sam DCruz/Shutterstock Images, 13; Manjusha Verma/AP Images, 24; Galyna Andrushko/Fotolia, 27; Rafal Cichawa/Shutterstock Images, 29; Antinolo Jorge Sierra/Photolibrary, 30; Andrey Plis/Shutterstock Images, 35; Fotolia, 37, 76, 92, 113, 121, 132; Jeremy Richards/iStockphoto, 43, 48, 128 (top); Robert Harding Picture Library Ltd/Alamy, 44; The British Library/Photolibrary, 50, 52; J.A. Mills/AP Images, 56, 129 (top); Govindasamy Agoramoorthy/Shutterstock Images, 58; Steve Estvanik/Shutterstock Images, 67; Marco Manzini/iStockphoto, 70; Girish Menon/Shutterstock Images, 75; Yuliya Kryzhevska/iStockphoto, 80; Jeremy Richards/Shutterstock Images, 82; Jack Qi/Shutterstock Images, 85; Simon Cooper/Photolibrary, 89; Altaf Qadri/AP Images, 90; Dita Alangkara/AP Images, 97, 129 (bottom); Rajesh Kumar Singh/AP Images, 100; Kishore Chand/AP Images, 103; Anantha Vardhan/iStockphoto, 104; Vikram Raghuvanshi Photography/iStockphoto, 107; Shutterstock Images, 108, 115; De Visu/Shutterstock Images, 116; Ine Beerten/Shutterstock Images, 119

BLACK HAWK MIDDLE SCHOOL
EAGAN, MN